"Great Faith . . ."

THIS BOOK IS DEDICATED . . .

. . . to all those who are seeking.
May this be a stepping stone
on your path to self-realization.

. . . to my brother, Bob,
who passed over on July 4th, 2000.
I love you. Thank you for your
continuing presence in my life.

. . . to all those who have come into my life,
to all those who are with me this day, and
to all those who have yet to share in my journey.
I love each and every one of you.
Thank you for making my life complete.

✥

In LOVE and LIGHT we LIVE!

"Great Faith . . . this is the title of your book."

✤

As I received these words, a book appeared before me in a vision. I could see from the book's cover down through all of its pages, but it contained not even one word. Yet I knew in my heart it held great meaning, for this is where my life's purpose met with God's plan!

CONTENTS

	Introduction
MARCH 6	"Great Faith . . . this is the title of your book." *1*
MARCH 13	My morning message *3*
MARCH 15	Open for business *7*
MARCH 16	God's word for the masses *9*
MARCH 17	God's test of faith *13*
MARCH 18	Open your heart *19*
MARCH 19	Be still and listen *25*
MARCH 20	Seek the truth within *31*
	The truth shall set you free *33*
MARCH 21	Free will *39*
MARCH 22	Your destiny *43*
MARCH 24	You are worthy *47*
MARCH 25	That little voice *49*
MARCH 26	The racecar driver *55*
MARCH 27	God's magnificent love *59*
MARCH 28	Your sacrifice to God *63*
MARCH 29	God's new world *69*
MARCH 30	Accept all religions *73*
	Soul journey *77*
	The open book *81*
MARCH 31	My question *83*
APRIL 2	Morning light *87*
	Never doubt His presence *89*
APRIL 3	Letting go *91*

April 4	Awareness 95
	Words of wisdom 99
April 5	He truly loves us all 101
April 7	Love 105
April 8	A union of spirits 109
April 11	Believe in the oneness 113
	The truth within 117
April 14	Reunite with the spirit 121
April 17	True wealth 125
April 18	A change in my heart 129
April 20	Be open 133
April 25	Faith 137
April 30	The power of love 143
May 2	Family ties 149
May 3	A test of my faith 155
May 5	The light . . . the life . . . the love 159
May 7	Where is your faith? 163
	The golden yellow light 169
May 9	And unto you a child is born 175
May 18	The all-knowing of God 179
May 20	Spiritual growth 185
May 21	God's most glorious secret 193
May 22	We hear you 197
May 24	Great faith 199
May 25	I AM 205

INTRODUCTION

I was introduced to God many years ago in a small church, in a small town. From that moment forward I have never doubted God's existence. I have always believed! Yet even at a very young age I knew that there was a complexity to understanding God's magnificence and that no matter what age I reached I would not in this lifetime truly comprehend it. For how can we? And because of that awareness I always remained open in my outlook, taking into my belief system all that made sense to me, all that fit into my picture of understanding.

More recently I became so much more aware of my desire to understand the truth. Not just the truth as I wanted to believe it, but God's truth. For I had finally reached a place in my life where the emptiness within myself, that part of my being that didn't feel complete, wanted to be satisfied. I realized that what was lacking in my search for the truth was my personal connection to God—an intimate relationship. I knew then that it was time to establish a personal relationship with God that would fill the void within me that had not been filled through belief alone. I wanted a relationship that was worthy, fulfilling. I wanted to truly feel God's love . . . to feel His love within my entire being. I wanted to live in the Light of God!

So I prayed. I asked God for clarity. I asked Him to share with me His truth and to allow me an understanding of His truth. I asked also to be surrounded by all those divine beings who could direct my will and align it with God's will, for I truly believed I could experience His peace on Earth, and I was willing to extend myself to whatever heights and depths my soul could reach. Most importantly, I asked God to share His love with me. I asked also for a true recognition of His love so I could share it with all those around me. Once again I prayed. I prayed that God would hear my prayer, and answer!

Then I waited. I wasn't sure how God's answer would come, but I trusted He would in time respond to my requests. I had to believe! And somewhere deep within my being there was this sense, this understanding, that if I just remained open enough to receive then I would be blessed with the direct assistance I had prayed for.

One day after lunch I had the compelling feeling to silence myself and listen. I returned to the table and sat down where I had just finished my meal, then closed my eyes and calmed myself. By slowly inhaling and exhaling —once, twice, then several times again—I was able to completely release all thoughts from my mind, finding a place of peace and quiet within me. I initiated no further thoughts, but remained open to hear. For the first few moments nothing came. Then, suddenly, words began falling into my consciousness like raindrops appearing from nowhere on a sunny day. As I became aware of the words and repeated them in my mind, an excitement drew from within me. Could this be? Could this possibly be a response to my prayers?

My next opportunity to listen came two days later in the evening. There was a silence in the house that seemed so perfect. As I sat calming myself in preparation to hear, the perfect silence was broken. Someone in the house began to stir, walking across the hardwood floor downstairs . . . to the dishwasher . . . then to the back door . . . locks checked . . . alarm set. Within that space of time I focused, trying to block out the noise. I was having difficulty doing so, yet I remained hopeful. A smile eased across my face. I looked toward the heavens as if I could be heard and said I'd try once more. Just then the words came!

"You will need to keep the flow of energy to relate to me."

Flow of energy? I had never said these words to myself, nor had I ever heard them expressed by anyone else before that I could recall. Flow of energy? This I could not dismiss as my own thought! An excitement once again swelled within me. I realized something beyond my comprehension was now at work in my life. I promised God that I would take this seriously . . . that I would come prepared in the future. I would bring something to write on. A journal, perhaps. My first journal!

The following day, just as before, I came to a place of peace and quiet within. Allowing no distractions, I listened.

The words came, and I wrote them in my journal. I even dared to ask questions. And the words came. Again, I wrote them in my journal. The responses were simple—short and sweet—but still profound. It was as if the words that formed on my paper knew my soul. Knew my soul better than I did!

As the days passed by and I sought out these precious moments in time, there was no denying that the words came from a loving voice. A voice that spoke with gentleness and kindness. It held an angelic quality in its verse that I did not recognize . . . that I did not recognize as myself! It expressed a personality all its own, not like anyone's I know whose feet touch this Earth. Yet this voice knew just where to touch me, sometimes even where my conscious mind did not want to go. It drew from within me all those little things I had wanted to stay swept under the carpet, and made me face them all. In time I came to accept this and understood it was for my own benefit.

As time pressed forward, I could see I was being led down a path of greater understanding, not only of myself but also of the world around me and beyond. I felt as if I was seeing for the first time things I had not seen before. And I found myself opening to God. What was manifesting within my heart was the relationship I had longed for . . . hoped for . . . prayed for!

When I look upon today, I see the relationship I share with God has been given to me through the love, guidance, and support of those in the angelic realm. I speak of those, of many, for the voice I hear *through the words I receive* is truly a voice of voices, not singular in its definition. It encompasses those I have come to know who live in God's realm . . . those who live in the Light of God. There have been times, though so few, that those who reside within this common voice have come forth to share individually, and it is a blessing to receive their words. Yet I know they truly speak in unison, for they hold the same truth, speak of the same love. It is with no doubt in my mind that this voice lives in the favor of God, for how else could it be?

The story I wish to share with you on the following pages contains all of the messages I have been given to share with others, plus dialogue directed to me personally, and journal entries of my experiences surrounding and feelings regarding the given messages. Even though I received messages for personal guidance for two months prior to those shared here, I was not prepared for what was given on March 6th, 1999, the date this story unfolds.

MARCH 6

"Great Faith . . . this is the title of your book."

It is morning, yet I do not know this for I am asleep. Still, a voice from within beckons. It calls out to be heard . . . softly, so quietly . . . here to impart a message, a morning message. Gently I am guided from the silence of my peaceful slumber with the words "Great Faith . . . this is the title of your book." Before my conscious mind can even comprehend what is being given, I see a book before me in my mind's eye. There is nothing on the book's cover. It is simply there, appearing translucent. Then, with no effort and seemingly no lapse in time, my eyes are drawn into the book. Each page I am able to see, but the book has not been opened! Each page, one after the other, I witness as my eyes make their way through to the book's end. But all I am witness to are blank pages . . . waiting to be filled, waiting for words. My eyes race back to the book's cover. As I continue my gaze, I am able to view the book from all directions at once, every aspect of it, as if my vision is all-dimensional.

My conscious awareness begins to establish itself, absorbing what has been given. As my thoughts take over, the book ceases to exist in the world of my conscious reality. But what remains imprinted in my memory is something I cannot deny. A realness, a truth, that I cannot describe.

I open my eyes to see daylight streaming in through the bedroom windows. I lie in bed gathering my thoughts. What could be dismissed as a dream is not. Somehow I know better. Yet what do I make of these words and this vision? I am not a writer, nor have I ever wished to be. And I do not have a book in need of a title. And what do I know about great faith? Surely if I were to write a book, I would choose a topic more familiar to me. Still, there must be some truth in all of this. I can *feel* it!

I know not to doubt, but to accept. My experiences over the past two months have taught me this. Even with all I still do not understand, I believe there is purpose in what has transpired. All I ask now of myself is to remain open.

with others. This is God's plan. Feel blessed! This is a great privilege which has been given to you by your Heavenly Father.

Look for inspiration in all around you. Others will offer their support of you. We know you are tired. You have been putting great efforts forward, and we are very proud of you! Yes, you can accept this praise . . . you are deserving. Smile upon yourself, for you have earned this right.

Always continue to increase your knowledge and understanding through your Lord Jesus Christ. He supports you in all you are doing in the name of the Father, the Almighty Everlasting God! Believe in Him always. We cherish your commitment made to Him.

You have done well. Go in peace. We love you! Amen."

clearly the words "Great Faith . . . this is the title of your book." I have learned to write them down immediately, for as I hear them, they so quickly, so quietly, step away from my being. And I do not want to forget them. I do not want to lose my connection to the world that exists beyond my conscious reality.

So once again without hesitation, I reach for the notepad on my nightstand and write the given words. On this morning as I turn over to settle myself in for a return to sleep, an intense feeling surrounds me, a strong urge to continue writing, yet I know I have nothing more to write on. I realize I should be keeping my journal at my bedside. I acknowledge to my guiding force that I will do so in the future but that for now I just want to go back to sleep because it is only 6:00 A.M. The intense feeling within me vanishes immediately, but slowly . . . quietly . . . returns. I can no longer resist its prompting and go downstairs to get my journal. After returning to my bed, I listen. I know all those present in the house, at least all those I can see, are still fast asleep. And the words come.

> *"Dear child, the time to receive is now when your mind is fresh and open. It is easier for us to communicate with you at this time of day. Later in the day, your mind is distracted with other thoughts and the flow of energy is diminished. Know we will not infringe on your sleep as long as you are prepared to receive when you awake. It is vitally important that the messages are clear, for you are to share all you receive*

MARCH 13

My morning message

*"Flourish in your sharing of
all knowledge and wisdom
received from God."*

My morning message . . . there it is once again, words quietly placed within me.
. . . words I have come to recognize as significant, words I now look forward to.
. . . words which are just there, existing before I awake.
. . . words that coax me from my sleep into my conscious awareness, before I can even begin my thoughts.
My morning message . . . inspiring, enlightening, foretelling!

These words—these messages—have come to greet me as I awake from my sleep almost daily now since that first morning, the morning of March 6th, when I received so

MARCH 15

Open for business

Last night I came into a state of awareness, existing somewhere between sleep and wakefulness, where I began hearing communications that I recognized as coming from my loving guides in the spirit. The messages were worthy, and I remember thinking to write them down in the journal by my bed, but sensed no urgency to do this. The messages continued and, understanding what was communicated, I would repeat them in my own words in my mind to reinforce what I was learning. I realized I was being allowed to witness how I receive knowledge and information from Spirit!

Many different topics were covered during this session, but as I gained an understanding with each one, it slipped from my consciousness. Just before falling back into sleep, it was revealed that the mind is a factory where words, thoughts, and ideas are manufactured. In the restful hours of sleep when we are calm, quiet, and open to receive, our angels come to work with us. During the day, many of our thoughts and ideas are actually memories of those things discovered with the help of our heavenly guides!

*"It is your destiny
to receive God's love."*

MARCH 16

God's word for the masses

True to the word of my angels I am awakened from my sleep early, so early that it is still dark and I must write blindly across the pages of my journal, feeling the way along with my fingers as the words are given. Until now I have always come for guidance at my convenience. But as I will soon discover, there is a greater plan at work here beyond my understanding.

The message ends precisely as my husband's alarm clock sounds. I read immediately to him what I have received, for we are both anxious to see what has been given. It is discovered to be the first message to be shared with others! Yet it ends with words intended for me personally, those loving and guiding words that I have come to count on in my life.

> FOR ALL: "It is your destiny to receive God's love! Do not fear the inevitable . . . God will show you the way. You will see the reward as you enter the kingdom of heaven!
>
> Cherish God's every word . . .
> for He is the force that binds you to His love.

*Never falter in your belief in the Almighty . . .
for He is the true believer of all things.*

*Join with us in prayer for your enlightenment . . .
for He is the answer to all prayers.*

*You must go forward now . . .
it is your destiny to achieve great things.*

*Never doubt there is room for you in heaven . . .
for God receives all who believe in Him.*

*Go in His name . . . find your way . . .
because God also believes in YOU!*

We have spoken. Do not deny what has been given you, for these are God's true words. Accept all you receive as God's lighting your way. You shall see then His glory for yourselves!
    Know we love you in the name of the Father. Peace to all forevermore! Amen."

It is here that the words continue, revealing the individual voices I have come to know from the angelic realm. There is joy within my being as I read these *personal* messages of support and gentle guidance.

"This is given to you for the masses. You have done well! Accept God's love and praise. He is here for you in all you do in His name. You shall never die, but have everlasting peace with your True Father, the Almighty Host of Angels! Amen."

"Share all you receive with others. It is your destiny which must now be realized. Feel blessed that God has chosen you to be a messenger in His name. Love the Father, for He is your giver of life, love, and true happiness. Feel His presence now and forevermore! Amen."

"See all good that comes from accepting Jesus Christ into your life. Stay with Him in your heart, Cindy, for He truly exists for you! Love Him and accept His help in reaching the Father, your true giver of life! Amen."

"You have done well today in receiving the body and blood of Christ. Cherish His presence in the core of your being! Amen."

"Peace be to you! We cannot help but share so much with you, for you are so open and willing to receive. It is your blessing to receive the word of God. Rejoice in yourself, for you are doing wonderful things for the Lord. You may now enjoy your day, knowing you have succeeded in God's eyes!"

MARCH 17

God's test of faith

Yesterday, just after sharing the given message with my husband, John, I slowly eased out of bed. Having taken only a few steps across the floor, I stopped. I couldn't believe what had been placed within my knowing at that very moment. So unexpectedly I had been given the name of the head minister of the church to which we attend. I knew instantly why. I was to take the message I had been given and present it to him. I felt a reluctance to do so. What would I say? How would I be able to share adequately enough all the wonderful experiences that have touched me so deeply these past months? Would he even believe what I had to say?

As much as I wished I could slip back into bed unnoticed and pretend this hadn't happened, I knew in my heart what I must do. As soon as I dressed, I placed a call to his office and left a message for him. Not knowing when his return call would come, I couldn't focus on my daily tasks. I couldn't shake the nervousness within that had taken its hold. Yet I continued to tell myself all would be fine, for I knew in my heart that this directive came from

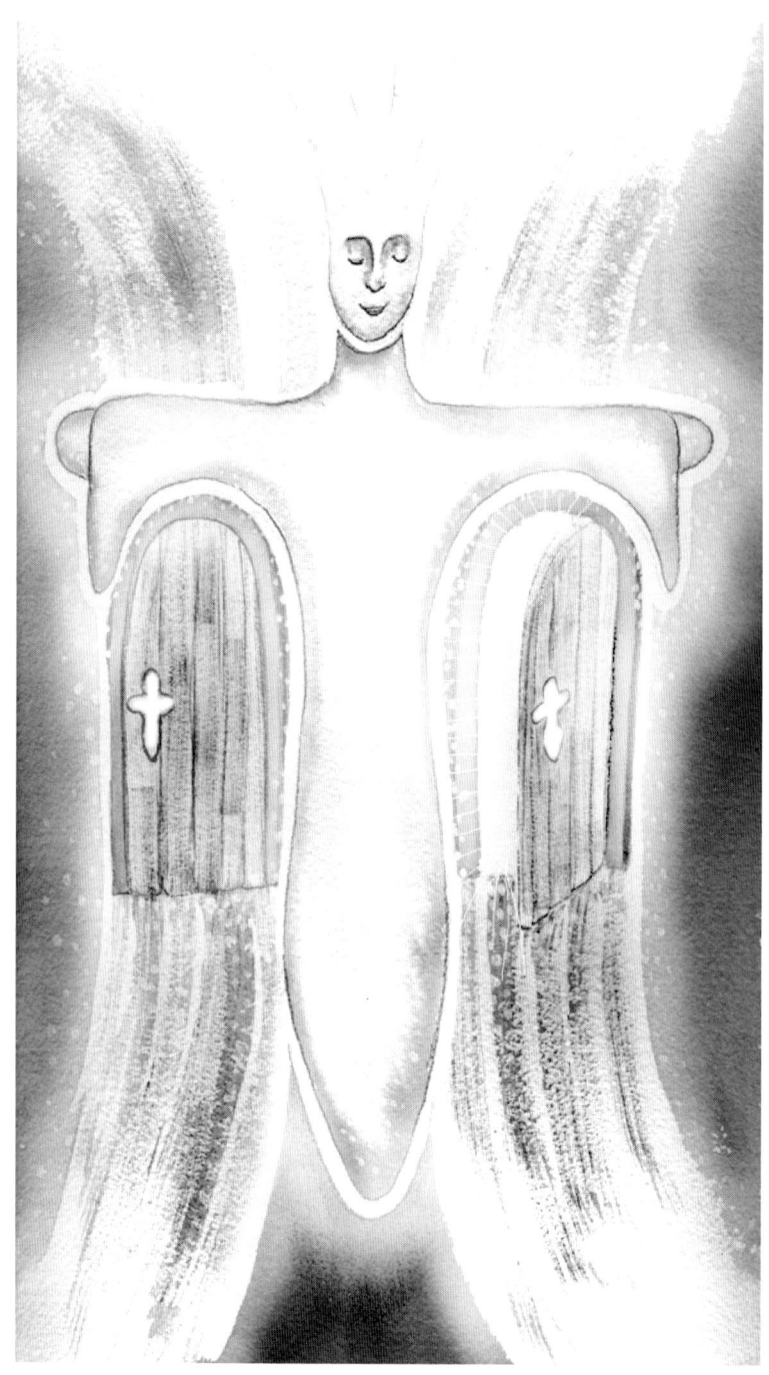

God and that there must be purpose in God's sending me to this minister.

This morning, more than twenty-four hours later, the minister's return call came. He started by asking me a few general questions and soon enough requested the purpose of my call. I asked if I could speak with him in person, knowing this would allow a more intimate setting for what I had to share. He stated his schedule was full for weeks, inviting me to share briefly with him over the phone. As I began to speak, tears welled in my eyes, carrying upon my voice. All my emotions came to the surface, not only from my apprehension of sharing my story but also from my awareness of God's magnificent presence which has been so beautifully active within my life. I very simply told him I have been receiving profound and inspirational messages recently that I know are not from me, but coming through me from a higher source. I made sure to say that I wouldn't be surprised if he had some doubt concerning their origin, hoping this statement would open the door for honest communication between us. He assured me that he believed I had had some sort of inspiration, yet he confessed that he did indeed doubt what I had revealed. He proceeded to make it clear that he didn't want to be bothered at this time, and suggested I just send some of my messages to him in the mail. I explained that they were too special and personal for me to send them but that I would be willing to share them in person when his time allowed. At this point he brushed me off, saying he had already given "fifteen minutes" of his time and didn't want to be late for his lunch date. Then he hung up.

I couldn't believe his response! I could understand his doubt, but not his indifference to my feelings and what I had offered to share. As I hung up my phone, I could no longer hold back the tears. I paced the floors, asking God why He had allowed this to happen. I just couldn't make sense of it all. I knew I could offer no proof to this minister of what I had revealed, which had been hardly anything at all, especially over the phone in a matter of minutes. And with that thought I so desperately wished I could have asked him how he even believes in God. After all, has he any tangible proof of God's existence? And the response I was given today comes from a man who continually preaches about God's miracles and how they are happening all around us.

An hour passed. Suddenly, a sense of peace came over me. In that moment I realized I had done nothing wrong. My only intention had been to share what I have witnessed personally as the mystery and glory of God. In my actions I had simply followed my heart, followed the direction I had been given by God. And with only another moment of reflection, my sense of peace turned to joy!

It is now evening that I write these words. As I return in my mind to the events of the day and to all the meaningful moments in my life, I must give *my* answer to the following question. How can we be sure of God's presence in our lives? *We know in our hearts!* We know from the little things that happen around us which we cannot quite explain . . . those little miracles in life that uplift us and bring us to a better place. With all my heart I do not doubt those little miracles. My heart is open. I just accept. I just believe. And that is great faith!

I still believe God had an intended purpose for sending me to this minister. Could it be God was simply testing his faith?

MARCH 18

Open your heart

As I open myself today to Spirit, I am blessed with words of love, encouragement, and guidance.

"Go into the house of the Lord, for He is with you. Let His face shine upon you! You have received well. God has not faltered in His sharing with you, for you have earned His praise and acceptance. He knows your desires to further your knowledge and understanding of His truth. Know you are blessed in the name of the Father.

Do not despair, for God is with you. You have been given a gift for all to see! Join with us in prayer for your enlightenment. We know you cannot succeed without God's love within you. Cherish His presence within the core of your being, for this is the body of Christ!

Do not judge others, for they know not what they do. You are open, and that allows you to see the truth you seek. Never allow your senses to betray you. Be thankful always that God has chosen you in His calling. You will travel a great many places in search of God's truth, and you will share uninterrupted in this lifetime. Do not fear this journey. Go now, knowing you have captured God's heart!

> *Peace be to you from us all! We love you. You are cherished for your open heart! Amen."*

Today's message means so much to me because it shows God acknowledges my open heart. When I first began communicating with those in the angelic realm, I was what I now call a mind-thinker. For the most part, I have always been a down-to-earth person—practical in my thinking, taking pride in my common sense. As with any new acquaintance, it took time to build a relationship with my angels. But even early on I could not deny the knowledge and insight imparted in their messages. As time stepped forward I came to trust in their guidance. And a relationship based on trust allows you to be more open and accepting.

As I opened my heart to my newfound friends, I not only received their words but also began to feel them. I could literally *feel* the emotions of my angels. I could sense their laughter . . . their smiles . . . their sincerity . . . their seriousness. But most of all, I could feel their love! At times I could feel it so strongly that I knew they were gathered all around, holding me in their loving embrace. I understood not only that this was their love but also that this was God's love! Through their love, support, and guidance, I came to understand just how real God's presence is in my life, for I could see it, feel it, sense it in so many things that happened around me. And through these experiences I found myself becoming more of a heart-thinker—learning from life's experiences through my heart's mind. With my angels' help I have truly come to feel connected . . . to feel *God's presence* within me!

Not long ago someone shared with me that he believed in God but that he hadn't yet felt His presence within. I think this is true for so many individuals. But feeling God's presence within is more than just believing in His existence. It is about establishing a relationship with God. A relationship built on trust. When you can honestly trust someone, it allows you to completely open your heart—allowing your vulnerabilities to show, not withholding anything—for you know this person will never let you down, never betray you. With trust, your relationship can grow. It can thrive! A relationship built on trust allows a connectedness, an intimacy, a love you cannot deny!

I thank my angels for their loving support and direction, for it is they who have helped me establish a closer relationship with God . . . to really feel God's presence within. Paging through the early writings in my journal, I see so often their guidance given in this matter.

> *"Feel His presence within the core of your being. This is who you truly are—God!"*

> *"Do not hold back. Feel all that is given you. Breathe it in . . . let it become you. Hold God's love within your entire being—every cell, every space within you. Open your heart, and you will receive all!"*

"Be open to receive all blessings from God Himself. He has so much to give. He will provide all you desire when you open your heart to Him. Allow Him to be your guide to everlasting peace, harmony, and love!"

"Come to Him with open arms . . . you will feel His embrace. God loves you! There is nothing you cannot attain when God is guiding you. Hold Him in your heart forever!"

"Just let go and feel the movement forward as you are being carried into the arms of your Heavenly Father. Rejoice!"

"Never hunger for His love. It is the breath that sustains your being! Open your heart to His glory. He will never falter in His caring of you."

"Never doubt His presence. Feel it in every part of your being. Feel it within your spirit, your true self. Do not deny His love, ever! Be open to all that comes, and so much will. It is there for the asking."

"You are so loved by God. He would never hurt you. Do not feel you must protect yourself. You can open up and let your vulnerabilities show. God will take care of you."

"Open your heart and let God expand within you! Let Him fill you with His love! Be true to yourself. Let Him reign within your heart."

"Be open and receive His blessings. You are now in the presence of the Lord!"

"Feel His presence now and forevermore! Amen."

*"Listen to your conscience . . .
it is your Heavenly Father's voice
within you."*

MARCH 19

Be still and listen

I am awakened this day at 5:50 A.M. Feeling the prompting of my angels, I reach for my journal and pen.

> *"We cherish your commitment made to the Father. Allow Him to bless you with His love. We know it is difficult for you to see just who God truly is, but never deny His presence. Seek His love and His way always. There is much to be learned by remaining open to Spirit. Keep His words with you at all times, for they continue to provide you with much inspiration."*

Still feeling half-asleep, I write their message in my journal. As I take what feels like dictation, my own thoughts flash between the given words. I cannot help myself from thinking the words being written sound familiar. And I wonder to myself, as I continue to write, if anything truly inspiring will result on this day. No thought can be hidden, and my angels respond to this immediately!

> *"Do not allow yourself to judge by what you believe are wasted words, for God does not give here for pleasure. There*

*is a definite purpose to all. You must believe that so sincerely!
Accept that God has chosen you to be a messenger. He needs
all those who are willing to do His work. Be open and receive
all! Do not shut any doors in your discovery of the True God,
for God wishes to enlighten all those who believe in Him,
and needs your help in accomplishing His goal. You are now
to share all with others."*

And with these words, a message is given for all.

FOR ALL:
*"Do not doubt the importance of God's love,
for He gives everlasting life to all!
He is the True God who gives life to the wretched, the weak,
and the lost souls of this world.
They need His love in order to be lifted out of their darkness.
It is not easy to see when pain and agony surround you,
when it seems there is no God who will save you,
but you have brought yourself to this place of loneliness.
God has not punished you.
Only you have punished yourself!*

*Get up . . .
look around you!
You must deliver a worthiness to receive God's recognition.
He does not force you to acknowledge Him,
but He waits eagerly in your discovery of Him.*

He does not judge you.
Only you are your judge, and you truly judge well,
for the truth lies deep within you.
It eats at you until you can no longer bear its gnawing,
and you then must let your demons out!

Listen to your conscience . . .
it is your Heavenly Father's voice within you!
It is a voice so powerful and guiding when you allow it to be.
Listen . . .
listen to the stillness in your being . . .
listen with your heart . . .
listen to all around you.
The birds, the flowers . . .
they dance for you in the breeze,
and the breeze is blowing for a new day which will come to you all!

Be patient and listen . . .
and God will find you!
Be open . . .
be patient . . .
and you will one day find yourself so near to God's heart.
He will smother you with His love
like a mother holding her infant child close to her breast.
Never despair, for God is always with you.
Know He waits for you all . . .
you are His children!

Be still . . .
listen . . .
you can hear the angels sing!
They give praise to the Father,
for they know of His beauty . . .
they know of His love . . .
they know God gives everlasting life
to all who follow in His name.
He does not forget . . .
He knows and sees what is in your heart!

So be still . . .
and hear the gates of heaven swing open for you!
God blesses you.
His face will shine upon you,
and your spirit will be renewed.
Accept all that has been given you,
for these are the words of God.
Be still . . .
listen . . .
God is coming for YOU! Amen."

"You now see, Cindy, the wonderment of God's word. He loves you and knows you mean well. You are not lost, but you are truly seeking His love. You are open . . . God sees that. He truly appreciates your commitment made to Him. Be still . . . for you are walking the way of the Lord!

> *Go in peace. Do not worry about what transpires here, for God will show you the way. Be still . . . you know in your heart He is with you!*
>
> *We bless you in the name of the Father. Amen."*

I read the message given today which is to be shared with others. I am not disappointed. There is such beauty that lies within—poetic artistry—that I know it does not come from me. These words reveal God's majesty, and I will hold them in my heart forever!

There is another message—a lesson contained within. When I received the sentence that stated I believed their words were wasted, I felt ashamed. I have never been let down by what I am given. Yet I worry whether the messages will continue to inspire and inform, for I have personally come to depend on these words in my life and never want them to end.

I now understand clearly that God does not waste His words but that He does reinforce what He says. Is it because we really aren't listening and taking His words to heart? I used to tell my children that I need to say everything *twice* because they only hear *half* of what I say. I wonder if this is how God feels.

God's words are not merely for our entertainment. They are for a definite purpose. So be still . . . and listen!

✢

*"You are loved for who you are,
but you will feel an even greater love
with an open and clean heart."*

✢

MARCH 20

Seek the truth within

It is early morning. At least it feels early to me, since I did not sleep well last night due to a cold. As much as I would like to return to my sleep, I know my angels are here waiting to give me a message. I can feel their presence. Just as I ready myself to write, the words begin.

> FOR ALL: "God is love! *Love is all that God intends for you to receive, but your ways continually keep you from finding His love. God does not punish you. You need to understand that so desperately! All the things in this life which give you grief are of your own making. Many of you choose not to see this, and that alone is what keeps you from His love.*
>
> *Calm your mind . . . open your heart! Look deep within and acknowledge the truth. You know the truth, the real truth. Face your demons so you may come to God with a cleansed spirit. Be honest. Honesty brings truth, and the truth shall set you free! God loves you and supports you in your self-examination.*

Go now in peace. You are loved for who you are, but you will feel an even greater love with an open and clean heart. Do not be afraid in your journey, for God will continue to walk along beside you on your path to finding His glory. Peace to you now and forevermore! Amen."

"Good morning, Cindy. You have truly done well today. We know it is early and your health is not good. God will cleanse you of those demons and you will be free. Expect to feel better! We look forward to sharing your day with you. Go in peace. Amen."

MARCH 20

The truth shall set you free

When I first began working with my angels, I not only was seeking spiritual guidance but also was longing to hear words of comfort . . . words letting me know I was in the right place. Yet there were times where the words I received hinted at truths about myself I had not wanted to see. Truths not so pleasant. It's not that my angels' words were at any time or in any way less than loving but that they held subtle reference to a particular reality within myself I needed to address. Sometimes it was not so much what they said, but what they didn't say, that was so evident to my senses.

    My first reaction during these particular moments in our communication was to suppress the thoughts and feelings that came forth as a result. It's not always easy to take a close look at oneself, but I knew these moments offered opportunities for growth and healing. I realized that it wasn't necessary for me to admit what I saw as my shortcomings to others but that it was important for me to really be honest with myself. For *me* to see the truth of the reality I had created within. As difficult as this inner

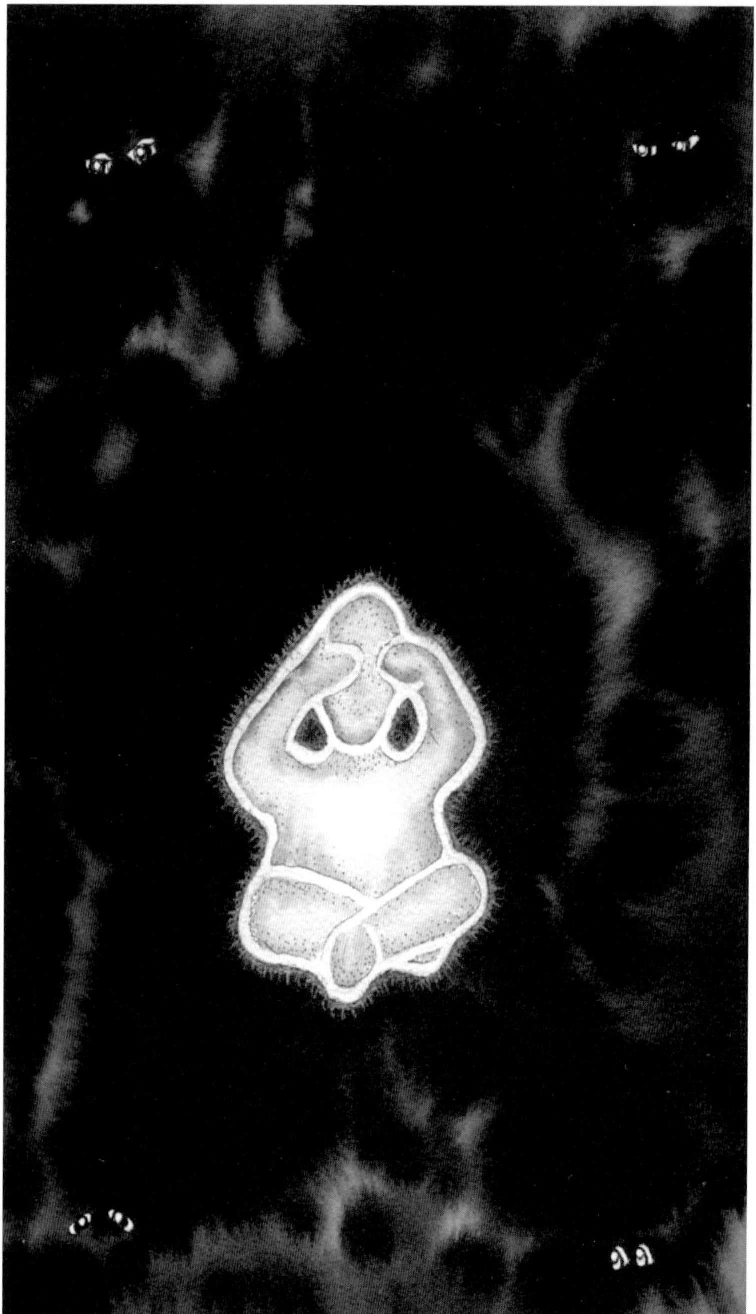

work appeared to be in the beginning, in no time at all I could see the positive effects on my life.

I know all of us hold a need within to know we are okay where we are at any given moment in time. And because that need can be so strong, sometimes we deceive ourselves by telling ourselves that there is no need for change. We're simply fine! It's hard for some of us to admit we can improve on ourselves, because then it's like saying we're not okay because we're not the best we can be. And no one wants to feel like a failure. So we live in denial. We do not look within to see what we can improve on. We do not do our work. We shut ourselves off and live in a world of illusion.

Denial keeps us from moving forward on our path of spiritual enlightenment. Denial is like saying we're fine where we are so there is no need to reach higher. Denial seems like a great place to hide, but what we are really doing is denying ourselves a greater existence.

When we step out from behind the curtain, when we choose to be honest with ourselves by taking a good look at all that lurks within our darker corners, we get a clearer picture of our potential greatness. When we can see who we now are and who we can be, we then give ourselves greater insight into *what* we need to change and *how* we can change those things in order to reach a more peaceful, balanced, loving place within.

We really are okay where we are at this given moment in time, so we can put away the fear. We can put away the fear because we can accept ourselves without judgment today, knowing, of course, that with an open heart and mind we will shine brighter. No one is expected to walk his entire path in a day. But if we can all walk with our eyes continually open, each day of our journey will be a blessing, for we will be at peace with ourselves and will be able to see that God truly does walk with us!

*"It is this power, your free will,
which God has blessed you with.
Use it wisely."*

MARCH 21

Free will

"Dearest Cindy, you are so willing to receive God's messages. Never worry about not receiving worthy communications, for God has much to say. We will proceed so you may once again return to your sleep."

FOR ALL: *"God wishes each of you complete joy and happiness in your life. It is your birthright to fulfill this dream. When you are sad, your spirit cries, and nothing positive can be gained. It is all about attitude. Your feelings are really choices, and you have many!*

Your mind is able to decide for itself all feelings and emotions. It chooses how to react to each and every situation which arises in your daily life. Emotions are not natural, involuntary responses to stimuli as you have come to accept and believe. Many of you seem surprised at hearing this.

Each one of you is truly in control of and responsible for how you feel about and react to everything you encounter. Think about it. You have the power to control everything you think, believe, and feel. What power! See then that this responsibility removes others from blame, for each one of you is responsible for your own destiny!

So where will you now begin? Begin by cleansing your spirit. Begin by asking God, your Heavenly Father, to fill your heart with loving thoughts. Ask Him to help you see your impurities and to show you a better way of seeing all that exists within your world.

God is waiting for you to ask for His help, but you need to come to Him. He does not force His will upon you. It is your choice, and you have many! And it is your choice whether or not you wish to be happy and not let your demons take control, for the control is yours. It is truly within you! It is this power, your free will, which God has blessed you with. Use it wisely. Pray to your Heavenly Father for His guidance and support. He is willing to help you succeed in all you desire. Desire God's way! Choose to allow Him to fill you with His love. It is all He truly intends for you to receive. This is His undying will—His divine will! And when you are open and willing to receive God's love, He can guide you to heaven. It is your choice, one which He hopes and prays you will make. But it is your choice. Think about it.

The gates of heaven will swing open for you if it is truly what you desire. Tell God what you want. He will guide you to paradise if you only choose it to be so. It is there for the asking. God will receive you. It is His will. Now He asks, what is yours? Amen."

"You have truly done well in accepting today's message. God is pleased you have chosen to accept His calling. It is also there for all who wish to receive it in His name. We pray that all who receive this message will hear His calling as you have!

Praise be to God, our Heavenly Father, that He has chosen to accept us into His kingdom of LOVE! *We are blessed . . . we are glorified in His name. How could we not choose Him! Amen."*

*"Never assume others
can do your work for you."*

MARCH 22

Your destiny

"You are your own destiny."

As soon as I awake enough for the words to register upon my conscious mind, I realize I have just been given a morning message. I write it in my journal. Then I listen, for I sense this is my angels' way of waking me so they are able to share a greater message. My senses do not betray me.

> *FOR ALL:* "So often people believe there is nothing they can do to control events and situations in their lives. But God knows this is not true. We all have the power to control our own destinies. Each one of you must realize this in order to cleanse your spirit for the Lord. It is your own actions which take you to heaven to be with the Father. But what have your actions been? What has been your mindset? You believe all you must do is believe, yet there is so much work to be done in your heart. Why would you assume that Jesus has done all the work for you and that you can just sit idly by and ride the train to heaven?

Stand up, get busy, for there is work to be done! You must now clean house . . . clean out the cobwebs of your soul. Do not despair, for it is not as hard as you might think. Just be open . . . be open to receive God's love. This is all He asks of you. Come to Him with an open heart. Come with an open heart which you have prepared not only through your belief in God but also by choosing to be responsible for your actions and your reactions to every situation in your life. You are responsible for yourself. You are responsible for your reaching the kingdom of heaven. You will never be alone if you truly desire this destination, for God does not wish the struggle to be yours alone. This is why He sent His Son, Jesus Christ, to walk His destiny ahead of yours—so you could see, learn, and follow. Remember, it is your destiny which you control. It is your life which you are responsible for. Never assume others can do your work for you.

Clean out the cobwebs of your soul . . . purify your being . . . cleanse your spirit! Truly walk the way of the Lord, and your destiny will not be one of lost hope. For God the Almighty is with you and will lead you out of the darkness into His light. It is a glorious light . . . seek it! Seek the light which offers everlasting peace, harmony, and love. It will never lead you astray.

Go in peace. Follow the Light . . . it will lead you home, and you will then surely dwell in the house of the Lord. It is your destiny. It is God's destiny for YOU! Amen."

"Good morning! We are so happy to share this message with you and others, for so many believe they need not take any responsibility in reaching their destination with the Holy Spirit. They do not understand the effort one must put forward to attain God's glorious gifts of everlasting peace, harmony, and love! We know how hard it is to teach others responsibility for their own destiny, for they believe Jesus has taken care of everything for them. He truly has paved the way to heaven, but we must still walk with our own feet to get there! We will help them understand. We will lead them down the path of righteousness and show them the reward in accomplishing their own goals.

Success comes from WITHIN! It is the blessing of Jesus who lived this truth for us so we could see more clearly the road to God's heart which He found. All is not lost. We will show them the way . . . you and I, hand-in-hand, with God's word to guide us!

Go dearly in peace, for we love you with all our hearts so sincerely! Amen."

❀

"Only you are your true master."

❀

MARCH 24

You are worthy

It is early. Much earlier in the day than I would like to be awake. I suppose in heaven the sun is always shining. That may explain why my angels seem not to notice that it is the middle of the night here! Oh, well.

> *"Dear Cindy, you are so good for being willing to accept these messages when you are still so sleepy. God thanks you for your undying commitment. You will never die of loneliness, for we are all here to give you our support! Please listen carefully, for we have good things to share with you. We will proceed so you may return to your sleep."*

> FOR ALL: *"The Lord says, listen to your heart, for it is your true guide! Do not let others influence your thoughts. Many of you know what is truly and indeed the right thing to do, but you allow others to make decisions for you and pass judgment upon you. You all have good minds and can think things through for yourselves!*

Trust in yourself, and you will never be lost or filled with doubt. As much as others wish to control your life, only you are your true master! It is not as difficult to be in charge of your heart and mind as you think. Trust in your own abilities. Trust in all you know which is true. Trust in yourself, and you will see you can truly believe in yourself. And why? Because God supports you and believes in you! He knows your true heart which is good. So lift up your eyes, see the shining stars, for they are the heights at which you can achieve your own self-worth!

It is really all about love! *Do you honestly love yourself? You do when you accept and trust your own heart and mind, and when you believe you are worthy in God's eyes. When you believe you are worthy, then you truly will be. God loves you. It is your birthright to love yourself also!*

So be still. Trust in yourself, and you will see many doors of opportunity opening for you. Go now in peace. Remember, YOU are worthy! Amen."

"*We know this message was a struggle for you, for you are truly tired. Return to your sleep now. We shall see you better rested in the morning. We love you dearly! Amen.*"

MARCH 25

That little voice

As I awoke to the early morning hours of darkness, feeling drained from the effects of the cold I have been battling, I chose not to listen for a message and returned to my sleep. But when I awoke some time later and realized what I may have missed out on, I couldn't resist making a connection with my loving guides from Spirit.

> *"Good morning! We are here for you and understand your desire for a good night's sleep, but remember that God has an important message to get out to all who need to hear, and not all of God's children are exercising their gift of hearing. You must act as their conscience. You are the little voice inside they need to hear.*
>
> *Do not deny your abilities a chance to thrive, for God has an intended purpose for all you do. We know it is hard to understand all that transpires here, but please remain open and continue receiving. God can then guide you to your next step. You are making great progress in coming to the Lord. No one sees that better than God Himself. Stay open in your faith. Allow God to orchestrate your every move. He will fit*

the pieces of the puzzle together for you. The way will be shown as you continue to learn and experience life.

We love you and pray you will always be here with us. We enjoy working with you as God's messenger. A great many things will come to you, and we are excited to be of witness to it all!

Go now in peace. Continue to pray for strength. God will never leave you. We know you now trust in Him and will continue to be open. Amen."

I am open. I listen. I trust. Yet it is human nature to doubt. I know about doubt because I have been down that road many times. Doubting came easy when I first began communicating with my angels. "Is this real?" I would ask myself. "Can I trust this voice?" I would even come to my angels and ask if I could trust their voice! They were so patient and understanding. And they would always give to me what I most needed to hear to quell my doubt.

Once the trust in my angels was established, I would then seek their advice on other matters in my life. But I was not always given what I expected to hear. For the most part, my angels do not give answers. Personally, I have come to know them much better for giving guidance. I must share a perfect example of this with you—the response I received some time ago after asking if it would be in my interest to seek advice on a specific matter . . . advice from a particular reliable source on *this* side of heaven. I have to admit, there is just something about hearing a human voice that is so comforting and reassuring! Here is that response from my angels:

> *"Dearest one, you do not need her guidance as much as you believe you do! You are so open and accepting, and that is all that is necessary. She could, however, shed light on your current situation which may offer you peace of mind, but you are very capable of trusting your own instincts in this matter. This is good experience for you, and so far you have done well. Believing in yourself is all you really need to do to find your answers!*
>
> *We know you would feel comforted in connecting with her, so don't feel a sense of guilt if you choose to use her help. But you truly can trust in yourself, which is ultimately trusting in God! We know you were wishing for a more definite answer in the positive, but we believe in your strength to trust your own wisdom.*
>
> *We wish you the best in making your decision. Pray to God. He will give you the strength and support you need so you won't have to doubt yourself. Be strong. You will endure. This is good practice for you!*
>
> *Go in peace. We love you and will continue to be here for you! Amen."*

How often do we seek help? Why are we so reliant on others? Have we become so conditioned to believe we must trust in and accept the authority of others that we have lost trust in ourselves? I know we have counselors, therapists, advisors, consultants, even ministers in the faith, all willing to set us straight. I do not deny that these individuals have a purpose, for they all have a gift to share. But even though we can find help and guidance for any and all areas in our lives, we can also find it within ourselves. Just think, our true strength and power comes from within!

There is a little voice. A voice so quiet and unintimidating that many of us do not even realize it is there. And many others choose not to listen to it because they do not trust it. It is easier to allow our minds to guide us, for that seems more real. But our minds are not perfect. Sometimes what we assume to be true really is not. Yet we want to trust the mind because it is all we know. We believe it is all we have.

Then again, there is that little voice. It is our conscience, our intuition, our gut instinct. It is our guide. When we learn to listen to it, we learn to trust it. We learn to trust it, for we see it never leads us astray, never disappoints us. It gives us direction and a sense of knowing. It gives us strength and confidence in our abilities. It builds character, and we begin to see we hold a power within ourselves that brings forth a sense of peace. With that little voice we discover our self-worth, which ultimately leads to self-love!

How can we not then trust that little voice, for it comes from such a wonderful place. It comes from within our hearts . . . from the love we know and feel inside. And our love is *God's love!* He is that little voice that reigns within. We can trust Him, for He never leads us astray!

I know how hard it can be at times to listen to and trust that little voice, for so many times in our lives we want and believe we need immediate answers. We are not patient. We want the answers now! But God knows what we need. And if we are willing to accept His guidance, He can bring us to a better place. So trust your inner voice. Let it guide you. The answers may not come immediately, but they will come. And it is the process itself, that journey through time, which will lead you to a greater understanding of all!

So be patient . . . be still and listen. Let God's voice be your true guide!

MARCH 26

The racecar driver

A few nights ago I had a dream. In my dream I was a racecar driver. The race was just days or maybe even only hours away. As I walked around I could see all the other drivers preparing for the race, making last-minute adjustments to their cars. Suddenly, feelings of inadequacy came over me as I realized how inexperienced I was! How could I compete with all those professionals? How would I be able to keep my car steady going 200 mph and not mess up?

As I was walking around trying to find my car, a good friend of mine came along. I asked him casually, not wanting him to recognize my fear, if he might like to drive my car in the race, telling him how much fun the experience would be for him. He gave me a sweet smile and replied that that just wasn't his sort of thing. Then, sensing my nervousness, he told me I would be fine. I was just to believe in my abilities and have faith, and all would work out. He had so much confidence in me that I couldn't help but find it in myself also. I knew that even as I stood there not being able to see the future all would be well. My dream ended.

Recently I have been wondering how I can write a book. I surely am inexperienced, for I have never written one before. Will it be worthy enough, and will I be able to keep pace with the more experienced writers? Even though it is hard for me to see how this book will unfold for I cannot see the future, I know everything will be fine if I continue to believe in myself, trust in my abilities, and have faith. The loving support of my friend in my dream reassured me of this.

Who was the friend in my dream? Who and what should I have faith in? For me the answers are clear. I believe everyone can learn from the guidance given within the contents of this dream. It is not really different from the guidance given through the messages I receive. And the messages I receive truly come from a loving and supportive *friend*. So as I share them with you, listen to all they say. For they truly guide us to believe in ourselves, to trust in our abilities, and to have faith in all above. What a wonderful place to *be* in our journey to God!

*"It is an unconditional love—
total, complete, without compromise."*

MARCH 27

God's magnificent love

"Good morning, dear one. God truly shines upon you! He will always utilize your talents, for you are so willing to receive. We have great things to share with you today. Be prepared, for God is always with you!"

FOR ALL: *"God loves you! He wishes the best for you always. Do not fear God's presence within you, for He will never demand more of you than you are willing to give. Be open! Find a way to give time to Him each day.*

There is a joy and peace within which comes from accepting Jesus Christ into your life. He wishes you all the blessings of the Father and will never desert you. He is filled with God's profound love, and He so desperately wishes to share it with all those who are ready and willing to open their hearts to the Father.

Believe They are here for YOU!

When you feel lost, the Universe receives your call. You are never turned away. Please accept and believe this, for God can then invite you into the kingdom of heaven. He wishes to fill His kingdom with all the lost souls of the Earth . . . all those who have no home within themselves for they have lost their spirit. God can fill your soul! He will fill you with His love, and you will be lifted from your misery and placed within His loving arms!

God responds to each call, for He wishes to teach love by example. He always offers His love. He would never judge anyone, for His heart is open. This is why when you seek God's love you will always find it. It is an unconditional love—total, complete, without compromise.

So be open, and reach for the stars! God is there . . . He is everywhere! Look around you. You need not look far. He is waiting with open arms just like a mother's to her child. He is there, standing at the doorway to your heart. Do not wait, do not hold back, for God is waiting for you! The reward is truly yours . . .

GOD'S MAGNIFICENT LOVE!

These words represent God's undying commitment to you. They are not merely words, but His heartfelt wish for all. Open your heart and accept Him unconditionally! Is He not there for you when you truly call out to Him? He is there in all you desire and receive. He is there in the laughter of a child, a cry of delight. He is there among those of you who gather in His name and sing His praises. God is in all things good. He is not judgmental. He is not wrathful. He does not punish. So rejoice in His presence!

Go in peace. God blesses you and will keep His promise. Go, seek His love . . . you shall truly find it! Amen."

———•·•———

"Praise be to God, for He has surrounded you with much love! Go in peace. Your day will be bright. Share all you know and receive with loved ones. Amen."

❈

*"God blesses you
continually with His love,
and now asks that you
open your heart to it
completely."*

❈

MARCH 28

Your sacrifice to God

I open my eyes to this day to see that I am blessed, for it is morning. Morning in the way that *I* would define it. Finally, a solid night's sleep! But as I settle in to the idea of being at peace once again with my blankets, I am aware that my heavenly friends are near.

> *"Good morning to you! We have been waiting for you to receive God's message from us, but understand your desire for rest. You need to also take time out for yourself. God not only wants you to commit to His cause but also wants you to enjoy receiving, for it is a joyous occasion to receive the word of God. Believe we are here for you at all times to give you God's word. We will continue to enlighten you this day. Do not fear, for all is well in the house of the Lord. Take the time necessary to fulfill your needs, as God needs you to be rested and willing to do His will. Continue in peace. We love you!"*

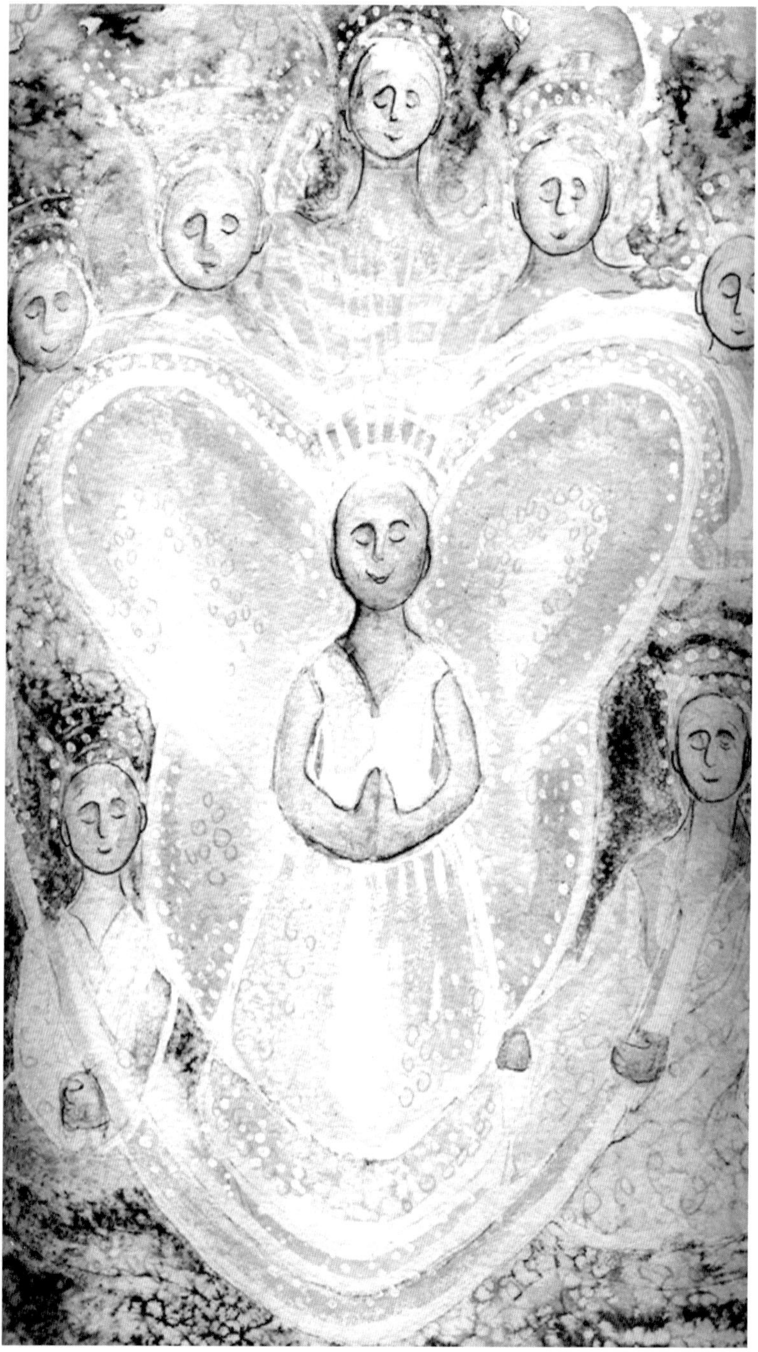

FOR ALL: "God wishes everyone to understand His desire for all to sacrifice in His name. It is not a sacrifice that requires devotion one cannot give, but it is one that will enlighten!

God believes each and every one of you has a gift to give when bringing yourself to the Lord. He has blessed you with this gift. It is the gift of love. Your gift is the same love that Jesus gave to all those He encountered in His life. God praises Him for He gave willingly and without reservation, because He saw the beauty of God's world, and He knew and understood His place in it. There is a place in God's world for you, too. But you are to make a sacrifice!

It is time to return God's love in honor of His commitment to you. God blesses you continually with His love, and now asks that you open your heart to it completely. God has a plan and a purpose for asking this of you. He wishes to share a greater existence with you, one which you will not deny as worthy. God does not misguide. He wants you by His side and wishes to show you a better way.

So listen to His words. The angels know to listen, for they see the glory of heaven. You are not so different. You can receive its glory, too. Just be willing to receive His direction unfaltering. Have faith in God's desire to direct your path to His heart, for He only wishes to lead you one way.

Feel blessed that you have captured God's heart. You will always be home when you accept and believe in all He has to give. Heaven can truly be on Earth, for it can reign in your heart when you allow LOVE to enter in! Amen."

"We so enjoyed sharing with you the message all listeners need to hear. Go in peace, for you have fulfilled your commitment today to the Father, the Almighty Host of Angels. He has many angels, even one which is willing to write these words. Smile upon yourself, for God is truly delighted in you! Amen."

✥

*"God wishes to give you
so much more
than you have been willing
to give yourself."*

✥

MARCH 29

God's new world

FOR ALL: "God seeks all who believe in Him. He does not wish to turn anyone away, for there is a new world waiting to be born, and God needs everyone's help and assistance!

Each and every one of you must look deep within yourself. Cleanse your spirit by removing all impurities within your heart by changing the attitudes you hold within yourself. Rid yourself of all prejudices. God does not judge you, and you have no right to judge others. God wants the pure in heart. He wants you to be open to all you receive from Him so He can show you a greater path on which to walk. But it is your choice. Do you want others to point the way for you, or do you want God to guide you? And who better to guide you than God Himself!

You must now open your heart in a much greater way to receive God's glory. He blesses you still for your acceptance and belief in Him, but truly wishes to take you beyond your world to a new world filled with greater knowledge and wisdom. This does not mean you must deny what you already know, but God wants you to be open to even more still, and asks that you find an even greater faith within yourself to *accept this greater truth. He will reveal more than you have come to know and understand in the past, and if you only choose to listen, He can open many doors for you. But you must be willing to listen to a truth you have not heard or acknowledged before, and God knows how difficult this can be. So God says, trust yourself! Trust your inner voice which you know is true. If you are truly open and willing to listen, it will not lead you astray. You will know in your heart what makes sense. And it is your heart which will lead you to the truth, for your heart knows all! It holds God's love within its beating, and speaks the truth with every sound it makes.*

Put your faith and trust in God. He will never lead you astray or ask for more than you can give, but He wishes to give you so much more than you have been willing to give yourself. Be open to God's way. Let God guide you to the new world He has prepared for you. Only you need to acknowledge it within your heart, and the mind will follow. All then will be understood, and the truth will be yours!

God is calling you. He needs everyone's devotion to create His new world which will exist within each and every one of you when you open your heart to it. Believe! Do not doubt . . . do not deny. God blesses you and keeps you . . . His face will shine upon you, and the gates of heaven will open to His glory for you forever and ever! Amen."

"Believe in God's choice of words. He needs everyone to see and understand a connection between what they know and what they need to learn. It is not easy to be open to new ideas that you have not heard or acknowledged before. Even those who have had many years to adjust their mindset are still learning. God's new world is just that. It is so new and intimidating to some, for they have been so set in their ways. They have not been guided to trust in themselves. They have not been told to exercise their own conscience. For their world wishes to control. It is the sadness of their reality. But what a difference an open heart and mind make! They allow you to take your wings and fly to a higher place in God's creation.

God wishes all to see, and needs you to gently guide their hearts and minds to the truth. You are their eyes. You will show them the way. You will lift them out of the darkness with the word of God, and the reward will be for all! Believe God knows what He is doing. Have faith and trust in the Lord. He is also your guide to everlasting peace! Amen."

What is God preparing us for? What truth does He wish to reveal? We can only be patient and trusting in His plan.

*"Open your heart,
even to all those you believe are different
than yourself."*

MARCH 30

Accept all religions

On this day I awake very early at 3:10 A.M. and sense I will be given a message. I make my way to the bathroom, then quickly return, for I can feel the excitement of my angels. A message is indeed given. When I look at the clock upon completion, it is 3:47 A.M.

> *"Good morning! Know we are here for you. You are such a faithful listener. God loves you for that as do we. Feel blessed as you continue with your writings. Jesus Christ is also with you. He loves you quite tremendously and is here to help you as well.*
>
> *Continue to keep your heart open as this day continues, for many wonderful things will take place. Do not feel discouraged by others who may not be so open to accepting these messages, for they do not understand their magnificence. You do, for your eyes are wide open!*
>
> *We look forward to sharing a very important message with you. Peace be to you. We love you!"*

FOR ALL: "God does not wish to turn away anyone who seeks His glory. He is open to receiving all believers. This is not based on one's personal belief system as many on Earth have come to accept and have been told to believe, for all is in God's creation. All religions are blessed by the Father. God has had many messengers who have been willing to do His work. It does not matter the formalities of their teachings, but that they teach the truth about God's love. This is what binds all religions . . . GOD'S MAGNIFICENT LOVE! It is at the heart of all creation in the Universe as you know it, but the Universe is even greater than you can see. There will come a day when you will be blessed with this knowledge, but only if you remain pure in heart, for God wants you to understand and accept His magnificence in order to be blessed with this all-knowing.

So open your heart! Open your heart, even to all those you believe are different than yourself. Accept others in the way that you would want to be accepted, for God loves all! Rejoice in your differences as we rejoice in all the varieties of fruit which the trees bear. Accept all others of different faiths because they are not so different from you. Look for similarities, and you will see many. But respect your differences as a way to further your own knowledge, for this will symbolize your growth!

ACCEPTANCE . . . TOLERANCE . . . this is the way of the Lord! Do not allow yourself to sit in judgment of others or of these words, for God gives all truth. Believe this message by opening your heart. God will truly shine upon you!

Go in peace, for God blesses each one of you, and sees no differences among you other than what is in your HEARTS! Amen."

"You see, Cindy, the wonderment of this message. It has been a long time in coming, but God believes all are ready to hear. Rejoice that you can deliver this message so clearly!

We love you sincerely and with our open hearts. Feel blessed, for you have many surrounding you in the spirit. We are all here to give you our support and encouragement. Never feel loneliness or despair, for we are always with you! Amen."

MARCH 30

Soul journey

I very easily fell into sleep after receiving today's message, and slept for some time until I awoke to an intense force surrounding me. I have felt this before and have never known what to make of it. No matter what, it always startles me. In the past I have been able to suppress its encompassing power. But not this time. I called to John, but realized he did not hear me. As this force surged into my being, I felt myself turning upside down from within, and I knew I was leaving John behind!

    Suddenly, I was lifted out of my body and could see myself below lying in bed! I was aware of my existence in a *spirit body,* but nothing about this situation frightened me. In fact, I was overjoyed with what I was experiencing! The only thing that caused me concern was that I could not move my arms from my sides. I looked around to find everything in the room just as it should be, only the faint light from the night sky lining the objects within. With only moments to make my observations, I rose up through the bedroom. As I approached the ceiling, I simply slipped through it! Into the attic I went, taking note of every board and nail in its construction. I proceeded through the roof, witnessing every molecule in view of plywood, roofing paper, and shingles. Finally, floating above our house with only seconds having passed, I could look down upon it all. Noticing I was well above the objects tied to Earth, I was finally able to move my arms out in front to steady myself, and continued on my journey. I knew not to think about home so I wouldn't be returned there, and I prayed to God to stay with me and guide me.

As I moved up and away from the rooftops, my eyes caught the rays of a shining white light far off in the distance, and I saw myself on a path leading to this light! The path appeared as a clear tunnel that contained within itself a delicate thread-like track. Proceeding forward, I worried I might fall off, for I was up so high above the Earth. Still focusing ahead as I sailed through its gentle curves, I gained tremendous speed and could no longer decipher those things along the wayside. Everything appeared more like computer-animated images than real objects. During this journey I was aware of the speed in which I traveled, but it seemed to have no effect on my being.

Eventually I slowed down to where all within my path became clearer. I found myself surrounded by incredible darkness, yet I could see beyond the immediate to infinity. Then I stopped, for I had reached my destination. I looked down to find myself hovering over an enormous shield in this vast region of darkness. Its magnitude was beyond comprehension. As if waiting for my arrival, this mighty shield spread open like the shutter of a camera on cue, yet slow and deliberate, seemingly with great intent and purpose. As I peered through its opening, all the while it growing wider and wider, I found myself gazing at a brilliant blue sky. Yet the excitement within me called my eyes into the farthest depths of my view, sending me tumbling down a magnificent mountain into its valley below. The sun, shining from somewhere I could not see and having lit the sky to its heavenly hue, danced on the lush green slopes of this majestic mountain, the valley swimming in the warmth of its rays. Basking in its glory, I wondered to what this scenery belonged. Feeling as though I had finally found paradise, I was ready to leave all that I knew behind. But just as I locked its beauty in my heart, this wonder ceased in my reality.

    I opened my eyes to find myself lying once again in bed. What had felt to be a very real out-of-body experience now seemed like only a dream. But then, just moments later, I felt several kisses being given one after the other upon my forehead. I looked up, expecting to see John standing by my bedside, but he was fast asleep. My heart fluttered with excitement. *Angels! I have been touched by angels!* All at once I understood, for in the sweetness of their gesture, they had blessed me with the truth of my experience. Thank you, God, for showing me that everything is all right in *my* world!

MARCH 30

The open book

While lying in bed, thinking of all that I had just experienced, my mind's thoughts eventually eased. Yet just when I should have drifted into sleep, I had a vision.

Once again presenting itself was a book. But this one was different from the previous book I saw. It was open, and the left page was filled with sapphire blue words that spilled over on to the right. There, I saw a hand holding a pen, writing. I could see from the elbow down to the hand, and assumed it was mine. The hand was writing with a beautiful quill pen, and just above where the book lay was an inkwell. Everything I could see was encompassed by a radiant white light, so brilliant and pure, like nothing I have seen before. As I looked more intently, it became increasingly brighter, and I knew it was heavenly!

Now, hours later, as I relive this vision in my mind, I see the hand is a right hand, yet I am left-handed. I am, therefore, led to believe the hand I see is not really mine. The white light represents God's presence, and the hand is of the Light. I know the messages I write are not of my own creation, but of God's, and they are passed from His angels to me. I, in turn, must share them with others.

MARCH 31

My question

As I reflect on yesterday's message, I am glad to have received it, for it confirms my belief regarding other religions. I have always felt that there is a place in God's creation for all individuals and that we should not judge what we do not truly know and understand. But in trying to understand where we as Christians fit completely into this picture, I cannot help but wonder then whether Jesus truly sits closest to our Heavenly Father above all other messengers, or whether He is equally valued in God's eyes along with all of the other great prophets. I do not know. I do know that I have been a Christian all of my life and that Jesus is the only one I really know. It is He who is truly my connection to God in this lifetime, and the messages I receive so strongly support this.

So how do I make sense of it all? Knowing I am a follower of Jesus, and not wanting to undermine His validity and true purpose for being here on Earth, how can I find peace of mind? I had to ask my angels to clarify for me this relationship between God, Jesus Christ, and the other great prophets. Here is their answer:

"You are not alone in your desire to know, for many seek the truth. Jesus Christ is truly the Son of God!

God does not judge, and sees all messengers equally in His creation. God has had many sons who have chosen to do His will. This does not mean that each did not have his own purpose. Each prophet was truly meant to touch his followers in a unique way, for this was God's intention. We do not always understand God's purpose, for He has many. Yet He does not wish to confuse us either. We just need to accept what we see in His creation as the All-Truth, and never doubt what is revealed.

Do not despair when you feel lost and seek knowledge, for we will answer for you as best we can. Go in peace, for you now have a better understanding of God's kingdom of love! Amen."

Yes, that is true. I now better understand God's message. It is saying the only thing that really matters is *love*. Beyond that, everything we believe, say, and do is just an expression of love. Or not! We have all heard the saying "Love is blind." Well, look how well we see through the eyes of judgment. When we step away from love, we have not far to look for a reason to compare . . . and to disagree . . . to dislike and to label . . . to put down, to ridicule, and to reject . . . to discriminate and segregate . . . to anger, hate, and torment . . . to fight and to harm . . . and to kill! Even a single judgment undermines love. I guess blindness then really is a blessing, for it opens us to the world of feeling.

To the world of *feelings*. What are your feelings? Must one always choose insensitivity toward others? Has the search for external power completely suppressed the power of love?

Jesus was a simple man, yet He was a rich man, for He understood the power of love. He lived that truth in His heart every day and shared it with all those around Him. His energy of love changed the world. If one man can have that profound of an effect, just imagine what we could all do together! Is this the new world we are hearing about?

Maybe there is only one way to heaven after all. Through the eyes of love!

APRIL 2

Morning light

As is true today, most of my messages now come within the early morning hours of darkness. I take to my pen, even though I cannot see the paper before me, much less the words that will be written. I only listen and write. When I am through, it is still dark. I cannot read what has been given, for I do not wish to wake anyone from his sleep by turning on the lights. So I place my journal on the nightstand and try to return to my sleep. But it is a hard thing to do, for there is the excitement of anticipation within me. I know the truth is there, just waiting to be revealed, but I must wait for the morning light.

Do we all lie in darkness? I believe for the faithful there is always an excitement within, for we know when we seek the Light, God's truth will be revealed!

❖

"God is in everything."

❖

APRIL 2

Never doubt His presence

FOR ALL: *"Do not fear, for God is always with you. He is always within you! Never doubt His presence. God is truly the absolute force in your life. He has given you life! You are of the Father. You are of the Spirit. You are of the True Spirit which is God the Almighty, Maker of Heaven and Earth. There is no denying Him!*

Stand up . . . look now around you! See His creation— its beauty, its magnificence.

> *Smell the flowers . . . they dance in God's glory, and the bees make honey which is, oh, so sweet. The trees bear fruit, and you drink from the pool of the crystal clean mountain waters!*

Do not deny Nature's wonderful, inviting presence and say it is not God's presence, for God is in EVERYTHING! Even in all those things you wish to believe do not contain His presence. God is even in all you still do not understand. But it is your choice that you do not understand, for have you chosen to truly open your heart to listen to God's word?

God's word comes in many forms and in many ways. *Be open to and accepting of all that you know deep within your heart makes sense. You will know. If you listen very hard, it will speak to you. That little voice within will lead you to the truth. Do not deny its presence, for it is truly God's presence within you!*

Go in peace. God truly does walk with each one of you . . . believe! When you can allow your doubt to recede even ever so slightly, God will be there to open up a new world for you. Just give Him a chance. See what He can do for you. Be optimistic, for God will never let you down. He is your wings which will take you to the highest mountain, the brightest star. You only need to believe.

God loves you so deeply. Do not deny HIM *with your doubt! Amen."*

"Good morning to you, dear Cindy. We have so enjoyed giving you this message, for so many need to hear it.

Praise be to the Father, for He knows just what to do! He has come to you to receive His word so you may act as a messenger in His name. Feel His glory . . . it is now upon you! Amen."

APRIL 3

Letting go

Last night I had a dream. My brother-in-law came to me and asked for my help. He wanted me to answer a question of his by using the guidance of my angels. He wanted to know if he should attend the funeral of a very dear friend. He made it clear that if I gave him the wrong answer then I would lose his trust in my claim to receive from a higher source of wisdom. I knew he would then reject all I had to say. This challenge, of course, made me nervous, for I didn't want to disappoint him. The dream ended.

I know the dear friend he was referring to represents the beliefs he has held for so long in his heart. When we are asked to open ourselves to new ideas, it is not always easy to let go of those from the past, especially when our old beliefs offered so much comfort for so long. But it is all right to do so. We are simply allowing ourselves the opportunity to *grow*. God understands that letting go of what no longer serves us might not be easy for us to do, so He asks that we only find a greater faith within our hearts. Our minds will then follow and the truth will be ours. God

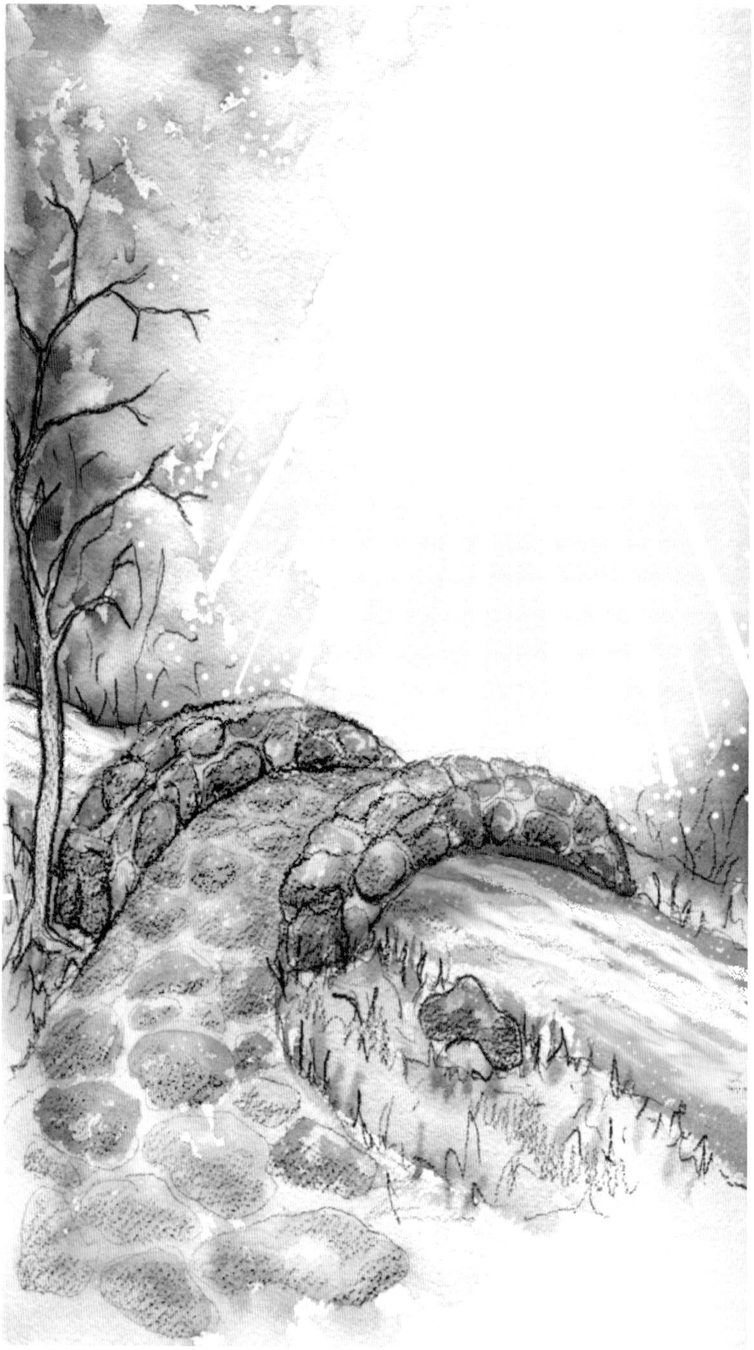

reassures us in His words. We are told of the new world that we will experience when we open our hearts!

I believe we need to give this greater knowledge and wisdom a chance, for no one can claim to already have all the answers. Do we have the audacity to say God doesn't either? My messages many times reveal that "these are God's true words." I believe. Do you?

*"You without God
are love lost."*

APRIL 4

Awareness

"Awareness is the reality of God's truth."

I hear the words—a morning message. Quietly they settle upon my mind. I know to wake myself enough to record what has been given. As I reach for my journal and pen, I note the time. It is 4:20 A.M. What more will be shared today, I wonder. I am sure we will learn about awareness. I sit in silence and listen. The words continue, manifesting upon my consciousness.

> FOR ALL: *"Awareness is the seed to which all else lies. And the fruit it bears is your freedom to express God's gift of realization. You only need to be aware to harvest the grandest of God's love and light. And with the knowledge of hope, you will see the glory of God's creation!*
>
> *There is really nothing to fear in opening to this state of consciousness. It only allows you to see the truth of all creation, and isn't that what you seek? Is it really so hard to open your heart and mind to accept new ideas? Is it because you fear change? And why? Your habits and beliefs are your safety net from the unknown, but the unknown is only your*

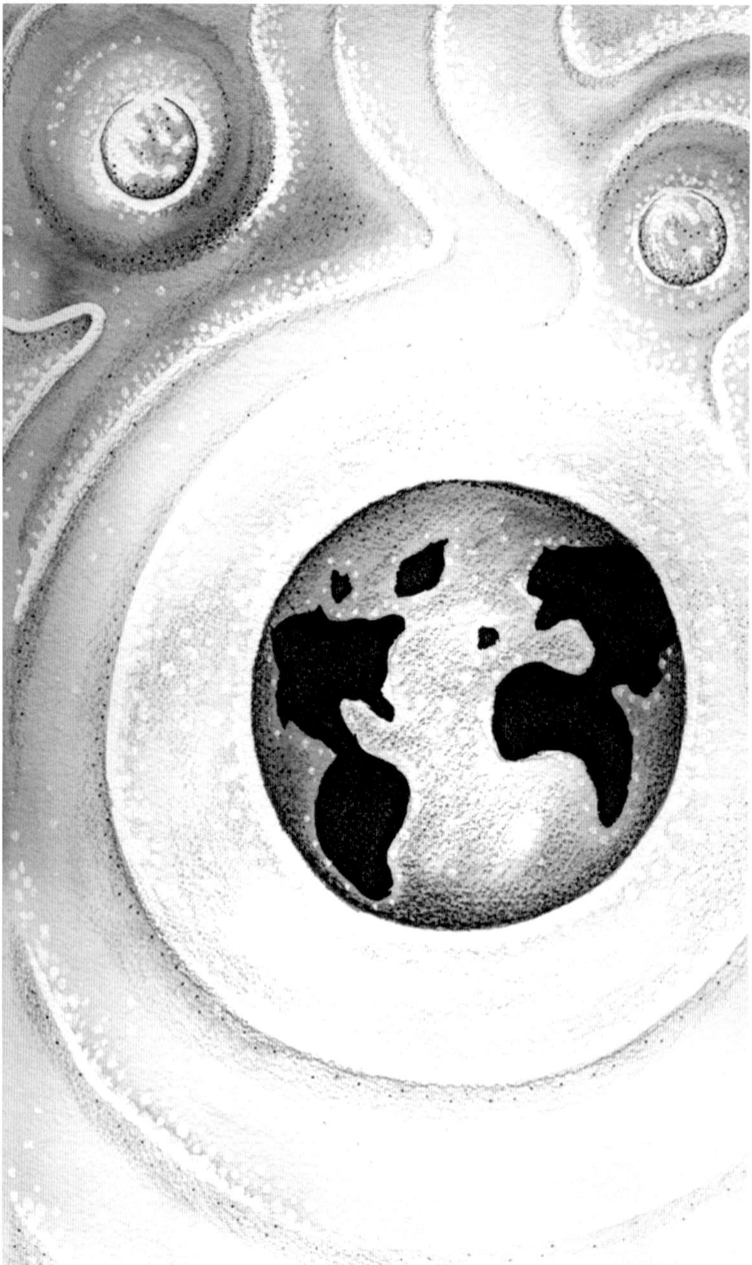

future with God. And why do you fear this so? Why do you cling to your ways? Do you really believe they are better than what God can give? We do not believe so, for we are aware! We live God's awareness every moment of our existence in the spirit, and you are of the Spirit also. You are of the True Spirit which is God, the Everlasting Greatness of all creation!

Do not forsake God by remaining closed within yourself, for you unto yourself would surely perish. You without God are love lost. You without God are only an empty shell . . . dead weight which would only sink to the lowest depths of the ocean floor. And where there is the light which would penetrate your soul? It is not! And there you would remain lost in the sea of nothingness forever. Is this what you choose? We think not!

Is it so much that God only asks you to open your heart and mind to the truth? You only need to be aware, and God will find you! He will come to you with open arms, and bless you with the love and security of His truth. Do not be afraid, for there is nothing to fear. Trust in the Lord. Be only aware by remaining close in spirit to your Heavenly Father. He will surely then lead you down the path of righteousness. Look to His glory, and you can only receive it!

God can guide only the open *heart and mind. Be open and clear! Wash away the darkness with your cleansed spirit. Joyfully accept God's wisdom. Let His strength give you the comfort you need to stretch your wings and fly. Hold nothing back! Hold only God's love to your breast, and it will be the wind beneath your wings. Let it uplift you! You will surely then soar to the heaven of God's greatest truth! Amen."*

"*Dear Cindy, you have such an open heart. Rejoice, for you have taken your wings to flight! God blesses you with His love everlasting.*

Go in peace, for you will always have God's heart in yours! Amen."

APRIL 4

Words of wisdom

A book is being written, but is it really mine? I am His hand . . . God is the wisdom. He is the wisdom behind the words that come when I rest my pen on paper.

When I seek to listen the words are there
    Only because I choose to be aware
        I never know what story will unfold
            I never know the truth that will be told
                I only know that the words will come
                    But not on which day they will be done.

Sometimes I feel like a blindfolded driver behind the wheel of a car traveling down the highway. I can neither see where I am going nor when I will reach my destination. Yet I know in my heart that God is my guide and that He will not lead me astray. For I have His word, and I have my faith!

"God turns no one away."

APRIL 5

He truly loves us all

Today I awoke abruptly at 5:50 A.M. to remember I had just been given a lesson on suicide. In fact, I felt as if I was still in the middle of it, because I could recall the last words spoken and some of the detail of previous things being shared. I thought this was such an odd subject to be discussing, since I had gone to sleep the night before with sweet thoughts of archangels dancing in my head. I read last evening how angels are just waiting to be called on by us for their assistance, so I had invited them all to be by my side! Later last night as I drifted off to sleep, I had a dream in which I saw myself in the midst of an impending disaster—a car accident. In the dream I immediately called out to Archangel Michael for his protection. Just after this scene I awoke to a sense of comfort, for I had instinctively known to do this. I felt my reading had paid off because the accident was not realized in the dream. And I was sure it was a sign that I am truly protected. I returned to my sweet dreams.

So why was I learning about suicide this morning? I felt there must be some reason for this, so I asked my angels for more information. Here is their reply:

"*You already know more than you think, for you have been studying. Suicide is not what it appears to be, and we must understand all in order to proceed. Many times the lost souls of this Earth believe they are not worthy of receiving any of God's attention. They allow themselves to fester within their own souls, and cannot find God's true glory and forgiveness in what they see as their transgressions. It is hard for us to understand the pain these individuals feel, for we do not live our lives grounded to the physical the way they do. Their insides ache with such pain and agony that they can no longer bear it. They feel suicide is the only answer to ending their pain, for they believe that God is not really there anyway to help them and that they will just die an uneventful death by slipping into everlasting stillness. But the world beyond is very active indeed, and this is much a surprise to suicide victims. For life goes on . . . and on . . . and on . . . .*

We are blessed with eternal life always from God, no matter who we are or what we believe our transgressions are. God does not punish us for being lost, because we are never truly lost! It is only within our hearts we believe that is true. All must realize this truth . . . God turns NO ONE away! We only turn ourselves away by believing God is not truly with us. We stop looking up to God's beautiful shining face, His glorious light, and instead look to the ground our feet heavily tread on. We are so earthbound in our misery that we do not see that from which we came. But we have come from our Heavenly Father who implores us to look up to see His love . . . His direction . . . His understanding. We are not lost. We have not fallen by the wayside. We only believe we have. And it is our beliefs which allow us to stumble and fall to the ground. God wants to lift us up. He truly extends His hand to all wishing to reach for it. He will guide us back onto the path by His side, and we will surely then reach the kingdom of heaven!

*God loves us with His entire being.
His heart is the Universe,
and we are the joy that makes His heart sing.
We, each one of us, are the love notes in His song,
and He sings continuously.
He needs each and every one of us to fill the Universe
with the heavenly music of His creation.
You are not lost, not even one of you,
so lift your hearts unto the Lord, for He is good.
He is good in cherishing each and every one of us,
for we are His own precious children.
He would not cast even one of us away,
for He loves us all.
HE TRULY LOVES US ALL!*

Go in peace, for you have God's heart. Hold on to the heartstrings which bind you to your Heavenly Father, and you will never be lost! Amen."

❁

*"The force that brings hope
to all eternity . . .
Love."*

❁

APRIL 7

Love

"Dearest one, we love you with all our hearts. Continue in peace, for you are doing the work of the Lord!"

―⋄―

FOR ALL: "God loves all! He does not turn anyone away. He sees what is truly within your heart, and does not deny you His love. Even when you are lost, He does not hold back this gift. Only you choose to deny it. And why? Do you not see the beauty which love possesses? Do you not see the strength that lies within?

Love is the foundation of all creation. It is what gives us life! When we seek to unite with God, it is the embryo which grows into true life everlasting. Love is the life-sustaining force of all creation. It continually radiates outward like the spokes of a wheel, weaving its way through all existence, through all things seen and unseen within the Universe. It creates the ties which bind us all to each other. Love is the sweet mother of joy and true happiness!

Love is all-knowing and all-empowering. It is the force that moves all within the heavens. It is the power which

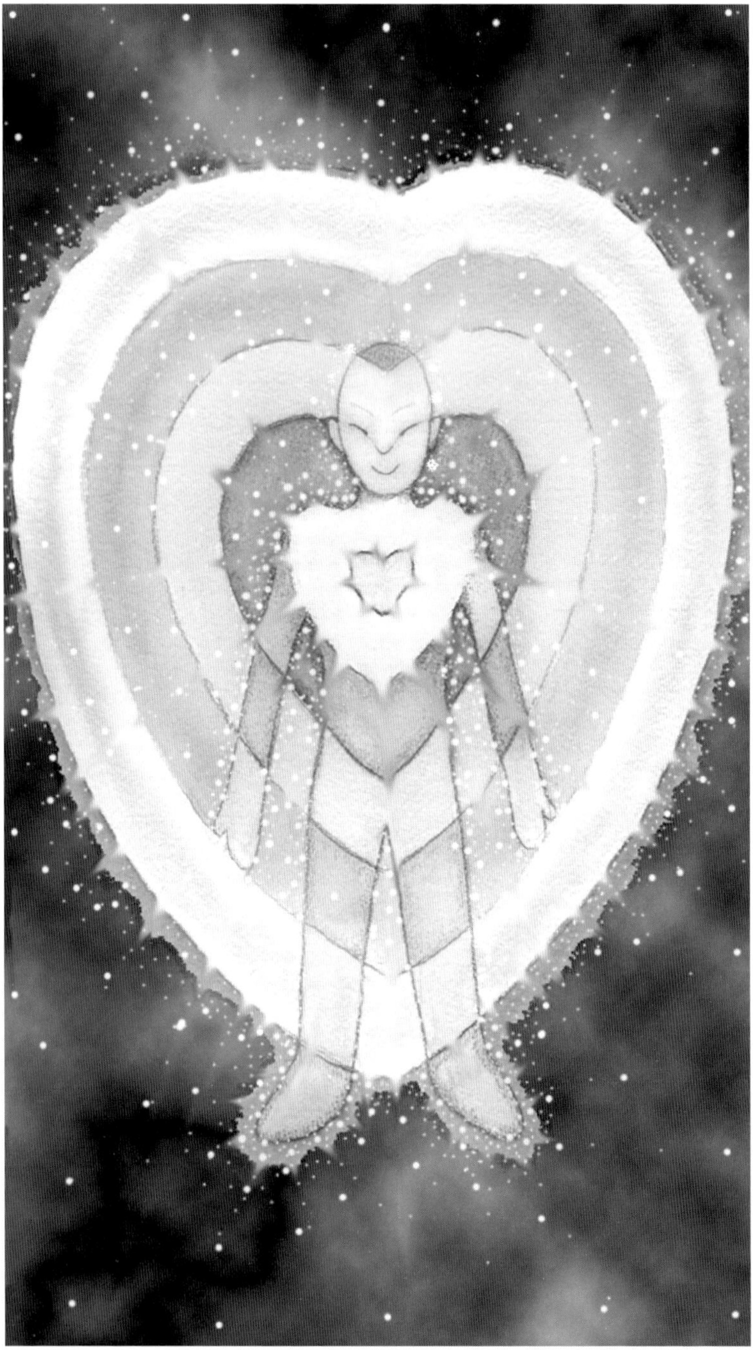

governs the Universe. It is physics in its truest form. It can never die. It moves continuously, for there is no force within all of creation which could ever stop it . . . for it is creation! It is God . . . it is light . . . it is beauty . . . it is the supreme wonderment of All! Love . . . simply love . . . the force that brings hope to all eternity . . . LOVE!

How could you ever then forsake God's love, for it is within you . . . it truly is YOU! You only need to realize this. No matter what you believe, you can never erase its existence within you. You can only choose to believe the absence of it within your heart. But what of the true absence of love? Its absence would cast a darkness over the land, creating a storm so damaging it would destroy humanity. Its absence would be the epitome of evil where all lost souls would hover within their own filth. They would be cast away in disgust, for they would be nothing without love. Is this the path you would choose for yourself, for it is a no-win situation. But how can God reach you when you hold back . . . when you deny His love? It is not God who casts you away. It is only what you do to yourself!

God loves you unconditionally and only wishes for you to receive His love. So open your heart! See the beauty of Love's light. Let it move within you . . . let it uplift you . . . let it shine from within you! You will never be lost, but you will truly find a peace within which only Love can bring! Amen."

❈

"When your heart
loves unconditionally,
you become One with God
in the core of your being."

❈

APRIL 8

A union of spirits

*"When you are with love in your heart,
the Holy Spirit never leaves you."*

Once again, a morning message. I appreciate these introductory words of wisdom. They are my guiding light, opening the door to a greater truth.

> FOR ALL: *"When your heart is filled with love, there is a presence within you which you cannot deny. It is a presence like no other. It is that of the Holy Spirit, God's True Spirit, and it moves you to act in a way that honors your Heavenly Father!*
>
> *God is always with you, but when you completely accept His love within your heart, there is a transformation. The pain and agony which once surrounded you is gone. There is an uplifting within your soul that moves you to God. When your heart loves unconditionally, you become One with God in the core of your being. This is a union of spirits—the union of your spirit and that of your Heavenly Father. It is a oneness like no other!*

Find God in your heart! Allow Him to flow within your being. Let Him be the rock on which all else lies. Let Him be the foundation of your existence, and all else will follow. God will be your support and guide in all your endeavors in this lifetime. God will be the true friend you have longed for. The loneliness in your heart will just slip away when your heart fills with God's love!

Let God fill you with His love! Let Him give you His gift of true life—the life of love He chose for you to live—not one of perpetual darkness. For God's love shines brighter than the darkest night. Its light can reach every corner within the Universe. We are the Universe. Love's light can penetrate us all. God's love can fill us all with the everlasting light of His True Spirit, the Holy Spirit of all creation!

God is love. Let Love light your way. You will never be lost. You will never be alone. You will never be filled with earthly pain and sorrow. For you will be filled with the hope and joy of all things good in the Universe which is God the Almighty . . . the mightiest of the mighty . . . God, the true power and strength of the Universe . . . GOD!

God wants you all to live with Him. He beckons you home like all good parents who miss the love and devotion of their children. Allow Him to bring your journey home . . . home to where His heart is. It is here where you will find peace and sweet solitude. You can rest your weary heart. God will comfort you. You will surely then be in the heaven of your dreams!

Come home . . . come home to your Father within your heart, and heaven which you have so longed for will be yours! Amen."

*"When you share your love with others,
you are indeed giving love
to yourself and to God."*

APRIL 11

Believe in the oneness

"Dear Cindy, know we are here for you! We do not wish to overburden you, and wanted to give you some time to reflect. We will always share the word of God with you when you come to us with an open heart. The words can never end as God is never ending. Listen once again to the beauty contained within these words."

FOR ALL: "God, the Almighty Everlasting Father of the Universe, is the All to an end and the beginning to All! He is the one and only giver of life . . . the One who has given life to all creation, to everything seen and unseen. He is the Living God. He is our Maker. He is the Creator of our being, and we are God in His entirety. We contain God, and we are God. God is the body of us all. We are indeed the love that comprises God's love!

Is it any wonder then that God seeks you so intently? Is it any wonder that God continually reaches out to you? God is whole just as a mother is whole when her children surround her. And what about the loss, the loneliness, when you are *away? God misses you! He misses the love and devotion you bring to Him when He is in your heart. How can you stay away, knowing of the bond of true love and life!*

God is One with each and every one of us. He longs for the union of our spirits, for it makes Him whole. And as we connect and become One with Him in love, we are One with all others in His creation. We are all children of God. We comprise the body of our Creator, for we in our entirety are the Creator!

> *Bless us, O Father, that we may see*
> *the glory of Your being . . .*
> *the glory of all Your children . . .*
> *our gift of Everlasting Oneness with You,*
> *our Host, our All.*
> *We, each and every one of us,*
> *are the total of Your love,*
> *and You are the True Love and Life of creation.*
> *We are All-Magnificent,*
> *for we embody the Love and Life of God Everlasting!*

When you seek God, you seek to reconnect with yourself, for you are not whole without Him. And you are not whole without all others in God's creation. How can you then forsake others, for just as you need God, you need the love of all those around you, because they are YOU and they are GOD! When you hurt others, you feel the pain. When you take from others, you steal from yourself. When you judge others, you condemn yourself. What is given is received! Is it any wonder then that your life feels so lost and empty when you do not hold love in your heart for others, for the way you see others is truly the way you see yourself, and it is ultimately the way you see God! So when there is love in your heart, there is love in your life, for when you share your love with others, you are indeed giving love to YOURSELF and to GOD! Giving is truly receiving!

We are all bound to one another, and there is no escaping. There is no you and I. There is only God. There is only the Oneness of all creation which we are all a part of. This is why you matter. This is why God reaches out to you. He is not whole without your love!

It is time to readjust your thinking. Cast away the thought of separateness, for it does not exist. Would God ever pass judgment on us, saying we are not all worthy? Would God sever His hand and say 'I do not need this'? The answer is truly NOT!

Believe in God. Believe in the Oneness. Believe in your Oneness with God. Do not cast yourself away. Come to the Father. Come home . . . you, with all His children . . . and bask in the glory of God! Amen."

APRIL 11

The truth within

As I opened my heart and mind to receive today's message, I had absolutely no idea what wisdom would be imparted. But as the story unfolded, it sounded familiar. The more that was revealed, the slower the words came and the more I struggled to hear. It was as if the words were coming from some place deep within my own being, more than just words falling upon my consciousness from somewhere else. It felt so strange.

When I received my messages in the past, because I was so intent on being open to hearing the words and writing them down, I could not focus on their meaning. In fact, I was never really able to understand the meaning of the messages until I went back and read them upon completion. This is why I always knew that they were not my words . . . that they did not come from me, but through me.

Today was different. As the message progressed, I felt that I was being asked to look within myself and follow along . . . that I was to be more of a participant than just a listener. When the message came to a close, I could not help but ponder the heaviness that had clung to its words.

It was as if the weight I had sensed as the words formed on paper was the weight of my responsibility for acknowledging their truth within myself. As this thought settled upon my mind, a greater awareness emerged from within. It was not the birth of a new idea I could call my own, but a sound truth as old as creation. Yet never before could I have as clearly understood this simple reality as I did today when my angels barely whispered God's words, challenging me to look within the core of my being for their truth. Now, a knowing that will always ring true for me . . . God's truth lies *within* me!

Today's message revealed to us just how connected we really are to God. And if we can acknowledge our Oneness with God, accepting that God truly lies within, then it follows we can also accept that God's truth lies within. But to realize God's truth and to experience its glory, we must actively seek it. We cannot only hope and dream that someday we will be handed the kingdom of heaven. We cannot assume that it will automatically fall into our laps. We must take full responsibility in our attainment. For the kingdom of heaven is *not* a place, but a state of mind. More precisely, it is *our state of heart*. We have been told previously in these messages:

> *"Heaven can truly be on Earth, for it can reign in your heart when you allow Love to enter in!"*

> *". . . come home to your Father within your heart, and heaven which you have so longed for will be yours!"*

We have also been told:

> "... God wants you to understand and accept His magnificence in order to be blessed with this all-knowing."

When we acknowledge that we are One with God, then we will understand that the greater truth of God lies within the core of each of us. It is already there, waiting to be discovered. We just need to open our hearts. This is the key to our success. We will then be *aware*. For it is through our hearts that we tap into the power and the wisdom of the Universe.

How nice it would be if the kingdom of heaven could fall into our laps by default. But I know God is showing us through the words in these messages that we play a greater role in our spiritual journey . . . that we are responsible for reaching our destination. God never says, dream on. He says, seek and you shall find. When we hear God's call, how can we not then open our hearts? How can we not listen to our inner voice? How can we not understand and accept the power and wisdom we hold within?

I know in my heart the messages I write are not of my own creation, but I am beginning to understand just how exactly the truth they hold also lies within me. What does this mean for us all? The wisdom we find within ourselves —when we choose to look through the heart's eye—is truly the wisdom of God. And it is this wisdom, *God's truth,* which will set us free!

❈

"It is He who you truly are."

❈

APRIL 14

Reunite with the spirit

"Dear one, we are so happy to be here with you once again. Never despair, for we are always with you! Listen carefully, for we have much to reveal."

FOR ALL: *"There are those of you who do not understand your purpose in God's existence. Your days are only filled with menial tasks which you succumb to. You busy yourself with physical pursuits instead of looking within to find your true self. You do not see yourself as connected to God as a spiritual being, but you believe that you only belong to the physical Earth plane. Yet this is not so. Your place in the Universe is with God, your Heavenly Father, and He beckons you to return to Him. You can truly live with Him while on this Earth if you choose, for you can accept Him into your heart and live His love. It is not that God will inflict His presence upon your life. It is only that He wishes to reunite with you through your acknowledgment and acceptance of Him, for it is He who you truly are!*

Why do you view your life as only yours, believing that you are separate from God and that God is just a nuisance to your otherwise eventful existence? Why do you seek to nourish the body and the mind, yet nothing is given to sustain the spirit? It is here where you falter. If you wish to believe that you exist only within the physical plane, then you should simply die at the end of your days and return to the dust of the Earth. But this would never be so, for you are of the Spirit always. Many of you still do not understand this and choose neither to acknowledge nor accept your true place in the Universe. God is the Magnificent Spirit, the Holy Spirit of all creation, and you are One with God. Can you not then believe you are truly of the Spirit? You are of the Spirit even today! Do not try to escape this truth. Look within! Do you not see your true self?

Your physical body is merely the trappings of your spiritual self. Your body is only the vehicle by which you roam the Earth in search of God's truth. Do not allow yourself to confuse your true nature. God wishes you to be joyous in these beautiful surroundings and to celebrate your communion with Nature, but remember that from which you came. For it is the glory of God which is your true home. Do not forget! Do not allow yourself to become so grounded to the physical that you cannot see the light of day. Do not look to the ground your feet tread on, but look up to see the light of God's shining face. Let it uplift you! Let God's presence lift you up into the realm of true spiritual living, for there is a whole world beyond that which your eyes can see. This is the world you truly seek in your heart. Is it any wonder then that you feel lost and empty when God is not in your heart? The yearning you feel is only for your true birthplace which is with God.

Remember . . . you are loved. God only wishes that you see and understand your place in the Universe. Find Him in your heart, and you will then already be home! Amen."

✥

"Let God be the joy you seek."

✥

APRIL 17

True wealth

"Dear Cindy, you have such a loving heart. Stay strong in your faith in God. He will lead you down the path of righteousness, and you will surely dwell in the house of the Lord!"

FOR ALL: "Do not despair, for God is always with you. He is the light that shines within you when your heart is clearly open. Never close the door to your heart by burdening your soul with physical distresses. Yet there are so many which you have created for yourself in this life. And why? It is not for the good of your spirit to be so laden with guilt, stress, and fatigue. You must look to the Lord for His reassurance and guidance that all is well within you. He can fill your heart and soul with the lasting peace and tranquillity you so long for in your life.

Trust in God . . . He knows what you need! He asks you to calm your mind and open your heart. Look for a moment of peace in your life and feel the goodness of it. Drink it in . . . let it flow within you. Do you not wish to always experience

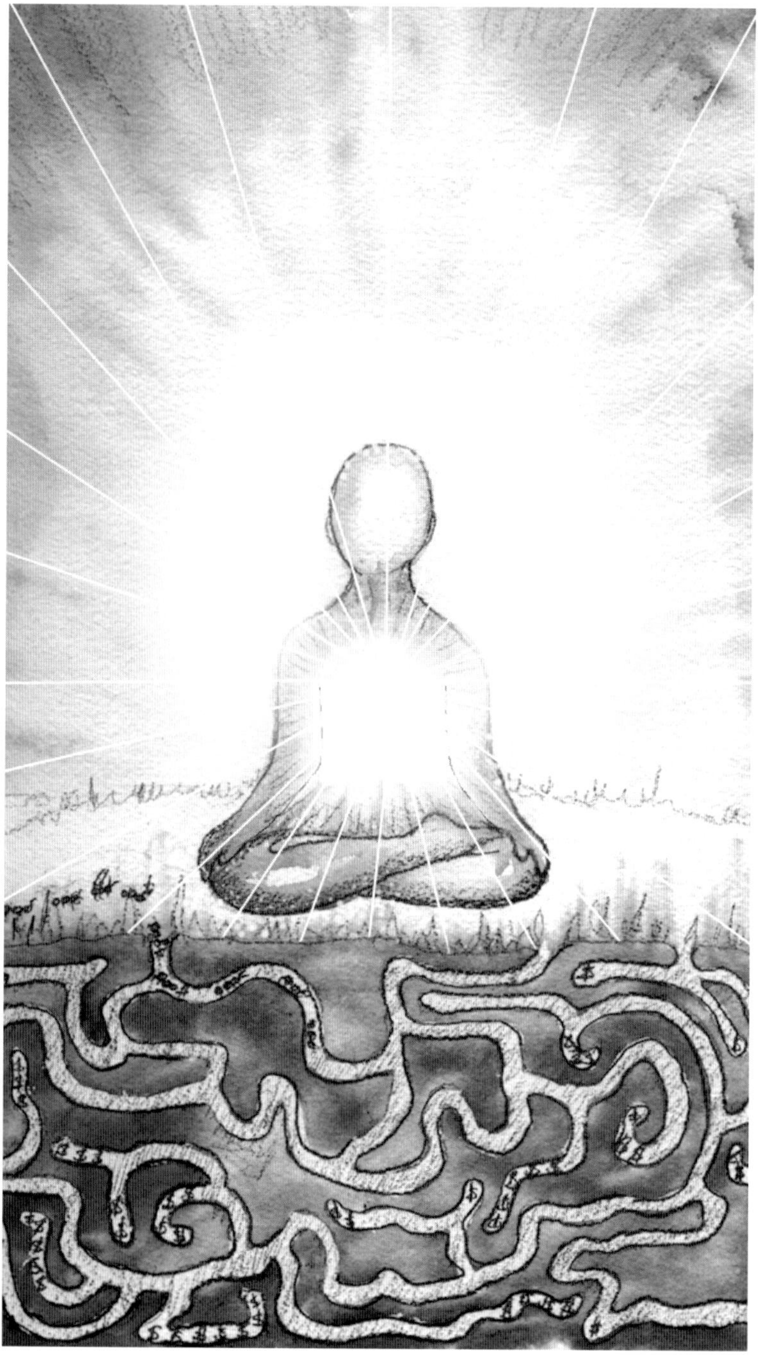

this joy? You can, and you will! But you must first make adjustments.

Focus on relaxing your mind. If you are constantly busying yourself, how can you truly experience the calm of peace and serenity? God does not wish for you to be scurrying around. Leave that to the ants of the Earth which have nothing better to do. You have purpose! Allow yourself quiet time to reflect on the purpose of your existence. What has your purpose been? What have been your goals? What has moved you to expend all your energies? Material wealth? As much as you would like to believe it is the means to your joy, you are sadly mistaken for it is not! It cannot fill your heart and soul like the presence of the Holy Spirit. Even with all of your material successes, the void within you persists. This is why your material desires perpetuate. For material possessions fill nothing but physical space. But you are not of the physical. You are of the SPIRIT! And of what substance will you be filled with when you meet your Maker? Only the memories of all your struggles and hardships endured in the pursuit of your misguided dreams?

God asks you to cleanse your heart and soul. Lift your spirit unto the Lord. He will give to you what you truly need. When you open to His will, all those things which you have given priority to will not seem so important, for you will then understand your true purpose. And your purpose is to reunite in Oneness with the True Spirit of all creation— God! God is your true giver of peace, joy, and happiness. When you allow that true connection with your Heavenly

Father, He will bless you . . . He will provide for you. You will receive His gifts . . . you will not be for want. You will be forever in the glory of God's creation. You will be at heavenly peace . . . you will have blessed calm . . . you will know true joy!

God does not ask that you cast away all those things which bring you happiness, but He does ask that you re-evaluate your priorities. God understands you are living in the confines of a physical world, and He truly believes in your comfort. He does not wish for you to be cold when the sun goes down with nothing more than hard rock on which to place your head. But when the light of morning shines in your eyes, be joyous that it is the Lord welcoming you from your slumber. Allow your actions and motivations within any given day to reflect the light that shines in your heart. Let God be your guiding light! Let God be the joy you seek!

Calm your mind . . . open your heart! Let God guide your actions and be your true motivation in all you do, and the wealth by which you judge your success will not be one of physical substance, but will be the glory and joy of the true heartbond you share with your Heavenly Father! Amen."

APRIL 18

A change in my heart

When I was a young girl, all I wanted for my future was to be a wife and a mother, and to have a beautiful house. In those early years I played house with my dolls, and my husband was the man on a postcard I possessed which I later found out was a picture of Elvis! Of course, *he* was always away at work, and I would tend to the children. My dream did not change all that much over the years, and even though I went off to college and brought home straight A's, I never felt my studies would result in a career.

    I did marry, and I now have a loving, supportive husband (not Elvis) and two fantastic children. Although my husband and I started out living life simply, over the years we moved up the ladder. Four years ago, we built a two-story home situated on two wooded acres. My childhood dream had come true! My children were already quite self-sufficient and I did not work outside the home, so my days were filled mostly with what I chose for myself. As peaceful as it all seemed, I still felt stress. The stress came from having to maintain a large house with all of our many possessions.

I began to feel a sense of burden by having to give so much of my attention to these inanimate objects. It's not that I didn't appreciate what we have, because I have always believed our material possessions are gifts from God. But there was this feeling that not all was right in my life. It felt like the lull before the storm. Here was my life, so exactly what I had wished for, but there was something lacking. For as nice as it was, I wasn't really being challenged. And I couldn't believe this is where God intended to let things remain. Of course, I didn't want to upset the applecart and step outside of myself, for when you aren't able to see what the future could hold for you, change doesn't seem so inviting.

I never believed when I started communicating with my angels that my life could change so drastically. Sure, it still looks the same to others. What has changed is in my heart. My angels have brought me to a better place within myself. I no longer feel tied to the physical world. In fact, I could easily give many of my things away. What I now have is a deeper love for my family, a more intimate relationship with God, and a true appreciation for His love, patience, guidance, and understanding. I feel blessed, and I thank my angels for their guidance and support in my spiritual discovery. I look forward to the future, for it is not a place filled with loneliness and uncertainty, but with love, peace of mind, and true happiness!

❈

*"When you remain open
to all that unfolds around you,
God can light your way."*

❈

APRIL 20

Be open

"Dearest Cindy, we so enjoy working with you this day. We love you and wish you success in all you do for the Lord!"

FOR ALL: *"God loves with an open heart. He does not judge anyone. He knows each of you is on your path to finding Him, and He looks to the day you will return to His side. God allows you to falter in your ways, for He is the Father who accepts and cherishes your commitment to Him. Whatever you choose is your destiny, for each of you has a unique path on which to walk in reaching the Lord. There is no right or wrong way, for all is meaningful in the course of events.*

Just as you strive to protect your being, you strive to preserve the Father, for He is the life force within you and the motivation for all you achieve, even if you do not realize it. As much as you may feel lost at times, all is meaningful and has purpose, for there is never even one moment wasted. If you choose to be misguided through your own decisions and mindfulness, then it is there where you will walk, for your way will ultimately serve as a learning experience and a lesson for you in the future when your heart and mind are more open.

Do not be frustrated with yourself, for everything truly has purpose. Choose to accept openly what is given this day. Do not be so resistant to all that unfolds around you. Take it with ease . . . breathe it in. Assume the responsibility for your experience, knowing there is purpose to it all. Be open to learning the lessons provided you in your daily life, for when you resist what is being offered you, you only block your growth. You bury yourself in regress. You challenge your senses by fighting your own inner battles instead of allowing yourself to progress to the next level of understanding and acceptance.

God wishes only that you keep an open heart and mind, for they are like an open window inviting in the warmth of the sun and the breeze of a new day. They are your connection to God in the clearest and most profound way, for when you remain open to all that unfolds around you, God can light your way. The sun will clearly shine into the window of your soul, and you will be blessed with the knowing that God is with you.

Never doubt, never fear, for God is always with you. Choose to remain open for the path on which you walk, and you will surely reach your truest destination! Amen."

❈

*"Faith is the key
to eternal happiness,
for it unlocks the door
to God's greater truth."*

❈

APRIL 25

Faith

"Good morning! We are here today to share an important message all would like to hear. Please listen carefully, for we have much to say."

FOR ALL: *"None of you are ever lost in God's kingdom of creation. He is with you no matter what you choose to believe. It is not always easy to see what the future holds for you, but your path can always unfold more readily when you are open to receiving God's help. He will choose always the best guidance for you, even though at times it may not make sense to you, because God knows the greater truth. He sees how you connect to all at any given moment in time, so He knows what you need in order to further your growth through greater understanding.*

Never doubt there is purpose to all that transpires. You are growing . . . you are living God's plan. When you choose to realize this, there will be no difference between what you allow for yourself and what God wishes for you. You wish to attain God's greater truth, and do so when you remain open to God's guidance. It is not that you must always understand His direction, but if you can trust in all He has to give, He can lead you to a better place. But you must have FAITH!

God grants all wonder and glory to those who believe and have faith in Him. Faith is the key to eternal happiness, for it unlocks the door to God's greater truth. When you lack faith, the door to your heart is tightly shut. The light of day cannot even begin to penetrate its seal. And God is the light that wishes to shine in your heart. When you shut out God, nothing of good can be gained. You become so grounded to your world and your ways of the physical that you miss all opportunities to lift your spirit to your Heavenly Father. How can you then proceed in your journey when you are sidelined by all physical deeds of your pious existence?

Open your heart! Believe in the Almighty power of the Living Spirit. Believe in God as your giver of life, the true savior of your soul. God loves you. When you believe, you receive. When you have faith, God hears your call. And a calling faith is. A strong faith in God is your proclamation, saying:

> I do not know all, Lord,
> but You are my Light . . .
> You are the Way!
> Please hear me, O Lord,
> as I wait in my darkest hour.
> I know You are there,
> for even as I cannot see You,

I can feel You . . .
I can feel You in my heart.
You are the Truth,
and I seek Your knowledge . . .
Your love . . .
Your understanding.
You are so great
and I am so small,
yet I know of the glory of my being.
I am important . . .
I matter . . .
and that is all I need to know to carry on.
Hear me, O Lord,
for I will continue to believe.
All the good I hold in my heart is for You,
and I will share.
I will come with my open heart to You!

I will carry my faith for all to see
High and mighty I will be
You will gather us by Your side
In faith we go, it strengthens our stride
We love you, dear Lord, with all we can give
And long for the day with You we eternally live!

God cherishes your faith, for it is your beacon you carry in the darkness of physical reality. And with that light you hold so dear, God can find you! You are not lost. You have shined *away all the doubt and despair of your soul. You are open to receiving God in His clearest form. There are no roadblocks inhibiting your growth. There are no thorns in your side gathered by wandering off God's path.*

> *You are OPEN . . .*
>   *you are CLEAR . . .*
>   *you are FOCUSED!*

Hold your faith high, and you will all be gathered by the Lord in His basket of Truth . . . and you will find the peace and serenity that only faith can bring! Amen."

✤

*"Tap into the river of love,
for it flows all around you . . .
it flows within you . . .
it flows through you
to all others."*

✤

APRIL 30

The power of love

"Precious one, we are here today to bring you joy and happiness, for you are so open to receive. We bless you with the glory of God, and we pray for your enlightenment. Continue in peace. We love you!"

FOR ALL: "YOU are a child of God! God cherishes you. He loves you and blesses you always. Be thankful for His love and devotion, for it is never ending. We have all been blessed with His gifts, for He is a glorious being! We cannot speak enough of His magnificence or even put into words the beauty of His love, but it is ENORMOUS! It contains the power to create endlessly, and we are all a part of that love. Never believe God has bypassed you in His awareness, for each of you is glorious in God's eyes. You are all His children, and He wishes to give you an existence of peace and happiness through love. Please be open to these wonders. Be accepting of His love for you and your worthiness to Him. Never doubt what He wishes to give you, for you are precious indeed! You are the beauty and the light that shines in God's eyes. You *are the music God wishes to hear. You are special . . . you are prized . . . you are truly loved and cherished!*

There is never a moment you have missed in the presence of God's glory, but have you realized it? The glory of God's creation has never halted, but only in your eyes. Do not choose to look the other way. God's heart aches when you do not look to this beauty. And why would you choose anything else? Do not sell yourself short. You are so worthy . . . you are so precious . . . you are so deserving—BELIEVE IT! There is no reason to doubt, no reason to fear. You must find the strength within your heart to carry yourself into the heavens. Enlist the help and support of others if need be, for it is all around you!

Love thy neighbor! Feel the bond . . . the kinship . . . the friendship. See the love they possess also, for they are you and they are God. There is beauty in all! Go hand-in-hand and march to the music within your spirits that you create for God's delight. God blesses the love you hold within for all others. There are no strangers. There are no enemies. All others are your brethren. Believe in the goodness of others. Look past their deeds if need be and into their spirit for the love and the light that is they, for it is there as it is in you! Choose to see it always, and you will never be lost and longing for love and friendship.

Look to the heavens also, for many are willing to guide and assist you. Believe you are not alone, ever! Those who have passed beyond your existence are still in your presence and are open to helping you if you are willing to receive it. Be aware . . . you will feel their presence! Listen . . . you will hear their comforting words! Look . . . you will see their guiding light! They offer their love and support in all you do.

And God's angels abound! So glorious are they to bring you great tidings of peace, joy, and love. They are God's truest messengers. Call . . . they will come. And to your heart they will render the magnificence of God. Believe! Trust in their power and their gentleness. Trust in their kindness and generosity, for they so much wish to give. But you must *call!*

Exercise your God-given right to be blessed with the support and embrace from all these loving creatures. They are beauty . . . they are light . . . they are the love of God! There will come a day when you will accept all and be accepted into all. Be open . . . stay focused. Feel the presence of God's gifts around you. Cherish all that is given you!

Only seek God's love, and you will find it! You will find it not only in God's heart but also in all the hearts that move to the rhythm of the Universe. Tap into the river of love, for it flows all around you . . . it flows within you . . . it flows through you to all others. It weaves its web of beauty like crystal catching the sun's rays—sparkling, shining, radiant, brilliant—reflecting the power and wisdom of God. Look only to see the love of God, and you will see all of creation . . . everything in and everything beyond . . . and your world will be limitless, endless. Its magnificence will move you beyond all realities, beyond all eternities. FEEL IT! *Feel its powerful vibration within you, the compelling energy it creates within your soul. How can you contain it? Let it burst forth! Let your love shine its ray to God. Let Him bask in the glory of your being. The love and light He receives from you will set forth an explosion . . . and God's newest creation of Love and Light will shine through all of eternity! Amen."*

✤

*"In our unity we ascend
to God's purest light."*

✤

MAY 2

Family ties

Even though I have not been graced with the voice of my angels quite as often recently, I was hoping last night as I retired to bed that this would be a day of rest. Today is my son Ross' Confirmation, and I had wanted all of my attentions to be focused on this event. I was so sure my thoughts would be honored. But as I awake at 7:10 A.M., I can feel once again their presence—that familiar excitement penetrating my being. I cannot resist this heavenly invitation, so I listen. There will be no regrets.

> *"Dearest one, we are so excited to be with you on this wonderful occasion, for your son is finding his way to God! He is welcomed into God's loving embrace, and we will all be of witness to that today. Cherish this holy event. We give our love to all!"*

FOR ALL: *"God cherishes those who actively commit to their Lord Jesus Christ, just as you cherish those around you who surround you with their love. There is a bond so deep which*

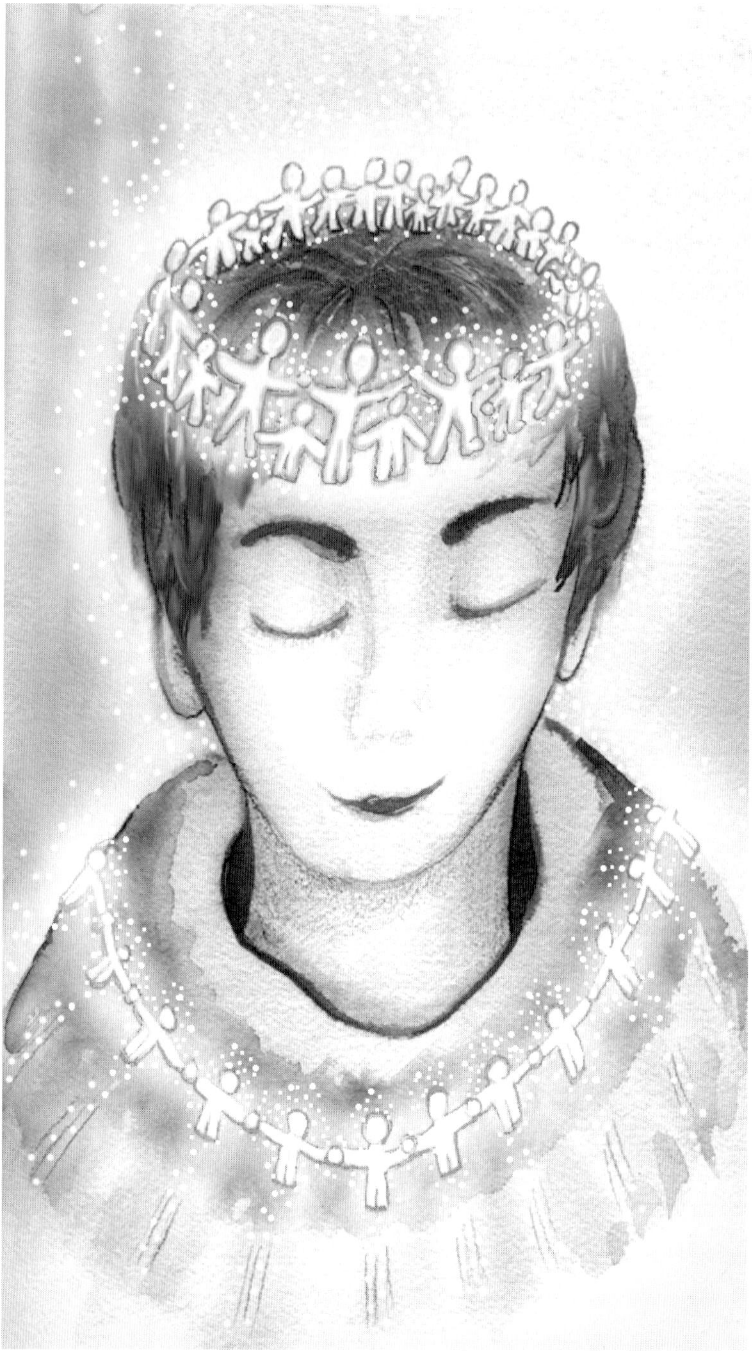

has carried you through eons of time, through many eternities. And you have chosen to come together once again in this lifetime to share your love for one another, and to support each other in your journeys to the Lord. You do not find your way alone, but you enlist the help and support of others whom you have created an everlasting lovebond with to carry you through. For no one can do it alone. Each needs the other . . . all others! Even when you believe you are separate and do not need those around you, you would be very lost without them. Yes, you want to spread your wings and fly, but that freedom comes from knowing deep within others will catch you if you fall. We are all bound in love. There is a melding of our souls, a uniting of our spirits. It makes us whole. And as we all come together in our love for one another, we come to God. As we share and give to one another, we glorify God's presence. In our unity we ascend to God's purest light!

God says, unite in your cause! Look to all those around you. Come together arm-in-arm, embrace within embrace, love giving to love receiving, for this bond will sustain you through all of eternity. And that kinship which is the glue to your existence will keep you together in warm, caring, cherishing love. Do not doubt or pull away from those around you who need your love and caring. Look past difficulties which may loom between personalities, for they are only surface wounds. They do not truly speak of the love connection between hearts. There is nothing which can truly break the ties of familyhood . . . of Oneness. It is only that others may be exerting the forces of their physical nature which may ring a sour note upon your senses, but these are not representative of their true nature. See the true beauty that lies within. Never judge. For no one upon this Earth can truly see the path that each of us walks, but we are all walking to greet our Lord. And you will see many times that your paths will cross and that you will be walking the road together. The road will not always travel lightly. If you can lift each other up, help each other along the way, then the benefit will be for all who shared in that journey.

Love all those around you . . . truly love! Look deep within their eyes to see their goodness, for the Lord is in each one of us. He is the Breath of Life . . . the Creator of our being . . . the Love and Light that is we! Welcome all within your family of love. Invite not only those warm, caring, radiant beings but also those whose light has been dimmed through personal trials and tribulations. Take in the lost souls of the Earth. Give them food and drink. Give the goodness of the Lord. Share your love . . . tend to their wounds . . . nurture their damaged spirit. Give cause for them to lift themselves unto the Lord. Be the light that shines forth on their path so they may once again find their way. Give, and you will receive! You will receive their thanks in friendship and love. The bond you create will hold strong through all weather. The family of love which you hold so dear will grow . . . it will multiply . . . it will reach out and expand through all space and time!

Reach out your hand . . . touch another's heart! The bond you create will be a thread in the loom of eternal life. And as your love-ties bind you to all others, a cloth will be woven—so beautiful, strong, and pure. It will blanket the Universe, allowing all to bask in its warmth and glory, and you will be smothered in the love of God's purest light!

Cherish your family of loved ones . . . invite all others in . . . and you will be blessed with the knowing that you are uniting in the SPIRIT of your Creator and truly living the Oneness which is God! Amen."

MAY 3

A test of my faith

Yesterday's events brought to my attention a story I have been meaning to write. As I sat at Ross' Confirmation ceremony, I was a witness to the faith statements given by six chosen confirmands. They were indeed inspiring and enlightening, mini-sermons in themselves. As I listened intently, I could not help but reflect on my own faith.

I return in my mind to March 17th, the day I was motivated to write "God's test of faith." I have thought many times since that day about God's intended purpose for sending me to this minister, the head minister of the church to which I attended yesterday. I know in my heart this minister is a good man, for I can see the amazing effects of his ministry, just as I could see yesterday its effects on those young hearts who spoke their accounts of faith. And God sees, too! Yet I know we all are human. We are all still finding our way. We have our ups and downs . . . our good days and our bad. So I must come to the defense of this minister who has not had a voice within these pages. Maybe on that one particular day, the day I was sent to this minister, God knew he was having a bad day.

And maybe on that particular day, God knew this minister—this man—would dismiss my words.

When I wrote that story, my intention was not to pass judgment, but simply to make an attempt to understand what had happened in those fifteen minutes, for when I hung up the phone I was hurt! And I couldn't make sense of what had happened. Yet I knew the time spent was meant to be, for I had so clearly heard this man's name being given to me after receiving the first message for others. So what was God's intended purpose?

I know the passage of time allows us opportunities for reflection. For growth if we allow it. And if I were to answer this question today, I would have to say that God was simply testing *my* faith. What if I hadn't listened to that little voice, the one directing me to this minister? Then what if I hadn't listened to my heart, for my heart told me that I had done nothing wrong and that I could trust in all I knew to be true. Would I really come to understand the meaning of the words "great faith"? Would this book even be in existence? If I had doubted instead of trusting my innermost feelings, maybe I wouldn't have been able to proceed in my journey with these messages. What then of myself and those readers who need their guiding words?

I know it is my faith that has brought me to this day, for when I was given the words "great faith," I did not yet have a book. And I had no idea at that time what this book would contain, or how its title would reflect the contents held within its pages. What has brought me here today is truly being able to understand that God's voice, that little voice within me, never leads me astray. I cannot say how this book will end, still I believe in all that is yet to be. That is *my* great faith!

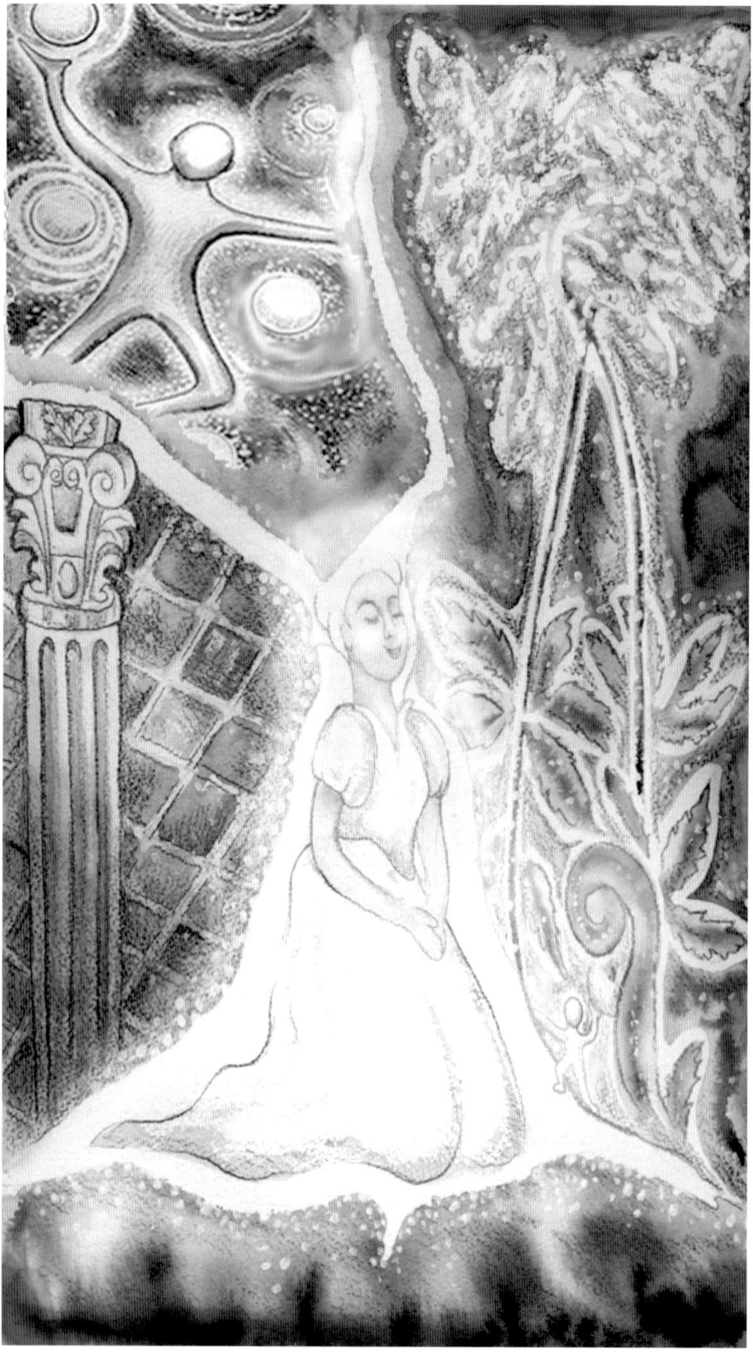

MAY 5

The light . . . the life . . . the love

Some time ago in the peacefulness of my sleep, I found myself standing in a room. A very large room. A grand ballroom with a ceiling so high and with pillars lining its perimeter—so ornamental, so majestic. I stood there alone, not in anyone's presence. Just I and the light . . . a golden light . . . a 24-carat golden yellow light! I was embraced by its warmth, feeling total comfort, absolute peace, and complete oneness. And I wondered about this light. Of what does it speak, for I believed God's light to be a brilliant white. Yet as I stood there basking in this golden yellow light, I could feel the goodness of the Lord, and I knew it was heavenly!

As time moved on and the sun rose higher in the sky—the days growing longer and temperatures rising— I knew it was time to go out to my garden to remove its blanket of leaves that had kept it warm throughout the cold winter months. I always enjoy this task each spring, for this unveiling reveals new growth . . . new life. I am amazed at what is uncovered. Just these tiny sprouts searching for the light—their sustenance. As the day drew to a close, I stood there gazing at my garden in anticipation of all that it is meant to be.

That night within the quiet of my being, I found myself once again at my garden, gazing in anticipation. My eyes fell upon the beginnings of an astilbe, its sprouts no more than half an inch or so. I stood there admiring its simple beauty. Suddenly, my eyes were drawn closer and closer to its being, and as they were, this life reached outward and upward toward me! It grew and grew all within moments . . . past me, around me . . . until I felt as small as a little bug down in the Earth within a forest of greenery. I was surrounded by its mighty stems—so strong, so full of life. I felt its energy, its aliveness. It was life itself! It encompassed my being, and I felt our connection . . . our oneness. We were one—this plant and I—living, growing, thriving!

Just a week ago during my sleep, I found myself once again in a room. This one was different from the last one. It was longer and narrower, emitting a soft, warm glow. I stood there alone. As my eyes wandered down the long corridor of this room, I saw lights . . . spheres of light . . . *angels* coming toward me! The light of each angel was encased in a clear globe. As they came forth I ran to them in such excitement, raising my hands, palms upward, to greet them. Each one came to touch me, rebounding softly into the air and hovering all around. So many of them! I knew to be gentle, and understood that the clear globes surrounding them were there so I could interact with them all. For how would I have touched only their light?

We played and danced, and the excitement within me never diminished, for we were together as one, these angels and I. I felt the blessings of their love from the joy within my heart!

What of these experiences that have been brought to me during my quiet hours of sleep? Do they foretell of the future, of a world beyond? Or do they speak of the present, of the here and now? I do not know. I do know God is always with us. If only we are aware, if only we seek, we will find the glory of His being. We are growing. We are reaching out to God. And even though it is sometimes hard for us to see, to witness through human eyes, God sees . . . He knows. And when we look forward in our faith, we are greeted by all those wishing to help us. There are so many!

*"Find your strength within.
It is only there
if you choose it to be so."*

MAY 7

Where is your faith?

"Good morning to you! We are here today to bring you a glorious message. We wish to share with you a message of hope. Please remain open as always, for we have much to say."

FOR ALL:
*"You are always with your Heavenly Father.
He is by your side,
even when you cannot see,
even when you find it hard to believe.
There is never a time when you are
walking down the road of eternal life alone.
Even though at times you may feel lost,
you are surrounded by so much love.
We know it is hard for you to understand,
so difficult for you to see,
for when your heart aches
and sorrow surrounds you,
what else are you to believe?
You feel so lost and teeming with despair.*

You wonder how anyone could possibly care,
how anyone could even more so want to be there . . .
for you!
You say that you are nothing,
that you just don't even matter,
and that God surely must have better things to do,
for He is with all those deserving souls
who have been blessed,
who are worthy,
and He just doesn't have time for you.
So you trudge along,
feeling so alone,
believing no one cares.
Believing no one sees or notices your pain,
your heart-wrenching loneliness,
the ache of despair within your soul.
Why do you not see those gathered around you?
Why do you not feel their touch on your arm,
the drying of your tears?
Why do you not know we are here?
Why do you believe there would be no one
to care about you?
You are not lost,
you are not alone,
for you are a child of God!
You are His precious gem,
the love in His eyes,
His one and only you,

a blessing to His heart.
God loves you!
God cherishes you!
God is always with YOU!
Do you not see?
Have you not raised your eyes to the heavens
in search of your Heavenly Father?
Do you not look
because you are afraid you will not find?
Is it because you believe you are not worthy
and God has passed over you?
Why have you lost all hope,
no longer willing to try?
What has replaced the desire in your heart
to find your way?
Where is your FAITH?
God does not promise an easy road,
but He does promise you the glory of His creation,
and He offers you every chance to find your way.
If you believe there is no hope,
then it is because you have chosen not to try.
You have chosen to wallow in self-pity,
drown yourself in sorrow,
plunge into despair.
Stand up . . .
find your strength within!
It is only there if you choose it to be so.
Search your heart and soul.

Do you not see the beauty that lies within?
Do you not see your worthiness?
God sees . . .
why can't you?
You must now put the past behind you.
Forget it,
for it is gone.
Today,
tomorrow . . .
they are the hope of your future,
and your future is all you allow it to be.
If you dwell in the past,
then all you will see is yesterday's footprints,
and where will be the hope of a brighter day?
You cannot see the light of day
when longing for the dusty road just traveled.
Focus on your future.
You are its only hope.
You must believe.
You must have faith.
Not only in God
but also in YOURSELF!
God is always with you,
but He cannot take your steps for you.
He can only lift you up,
lighten your load,
when you try.
Pray for strength.

*Pray for His guidance.
He will never leave you . . .
believe!
Your strength comes in your faith.
If you only choose to believe,
then God can work His miracles!
Step out into your future
with eyes shining and bright.
You will see God all along the way.
He will be the stabilizing hand
helping you cross the rocky road.
Do not despair,
for as lost as you might feel,
hope is never gone.
Hope is the light of a new day,
the strength within your heart to carry on.
Never lose faith in yourself.
Never believe the battle has been lost.
Choose to go forward,
and you will never be alone,
for Faith, Hope, and the Love of God
will be your truest companions! Amen."*

MAY 7

The golden yellow light

Today I received a sign from God. Just a little sign showing me I am on the right track!

When I received today's message, I couldn't understand why my angels felt more encouragement was needed. For as I recalled the most recent messages received, they were all so inspiring and uplifting that I couldn't imagine anyone still feeling lost or down. I read this message several times, even bringing it with me as I sat down to lunch, hoping to read it one more time and maybe discover what I had missed. But something told me not to worry about it for the time being, and I was drawn to a book I had put aside some time ago. Just after opening its pages, I came across a story within. A simple story about the golden yellow light!

I had never read anything before about this golden yellow light. When I recounted my dream of this light only two days before, I did not know what to make of it. I only knew God's light to be white. Yet I could not deny the sense of peace and comfort this dream had left me with, and I just felt there was definite significance to it, the same significance I also felt so strongly with my other

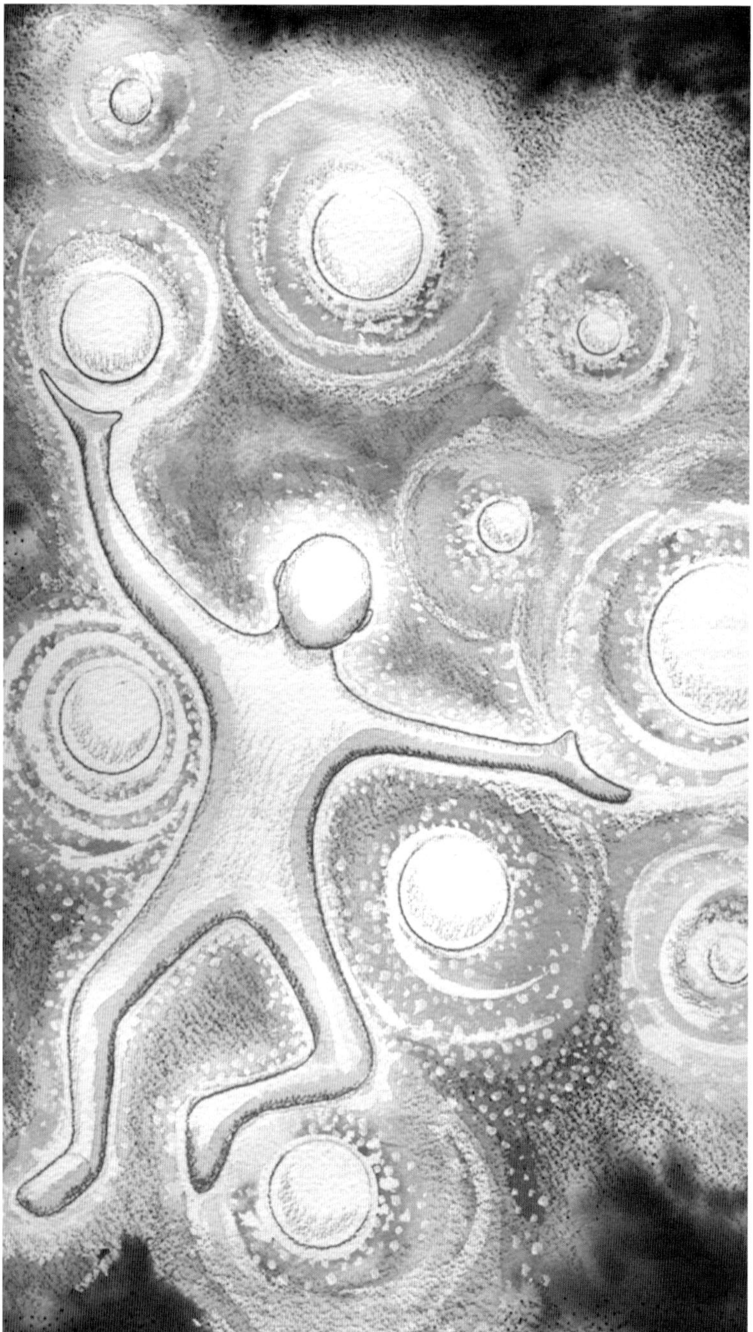

two dreams. As each dream became implanted in my consciousness, I knew a story was being revealed. Even though I can now see how close I came in translating the collective meaning of these dreams, I still did not understand the significance of the golden yellow light. At least not until today when I was directed to that story, and what a difference it makes!

As I read the story of the golden yellow light, it was revealed to be the light *we* possess. The light that shines from within ourselves when we, through our own efforts, spiritually connect to God. When we choose to go forward, when we truly make a conscious effort to be enlightened, we actually become *lighted* from within. Our spiritual growth is reflected from within our beings as light! And as we continue to grow spiritually, our light shines brighter and brighter, capturing the attention of all those in the Universe who see and appreciate its beauty.

So I feel blessed, for my efforts have truly been acknowledged! But I am not any better than you. I am not a saint. I make mistakes, and I make them every day. So I could question how this golden yellow light could even possibly reflect who I am. What I am sure of, though, is that I try. I truly *try*. Every day when I awake, I know I want to be closer to God. I want to feel a little more contentment within . . . a little more peace, joy, and love! So I continue to try. And isn't that what today's message revealed?

If we only try, if we only believe and have faith in ourselves, then we have hope. Maybe it isn't as hard as we all imagine. For not only is there hope when we try, there is GOD! Isn't He really the light that shines from within us when we open our hearts?

> Only seek to find and you will see
> > The Light, the Life, the Love that is HE
> > > The Light, the Life, the Love that is WE!

*"Through His love
you shall find your way."*

MAY 9

And unto you a child is born

"Faith is the stabilizing force in your life."

The words summon me from my sleep. *Hurry . . . write them down . . . don't forget,* I think to myself. I wake up a little more, and reach for paper and pen. My clock is also there, waiting to tell me the time. It is 3:15 A.M. I am surprised to see that when I write this morning's message the words continue to flow. There is no pause, no hesitation, no break in thought. Could this be a message in itself?

> FOR ALL: . . . *"It is your clearest connection to God. You cannot move forward in your spiritual growth without faith. It is the tie that binds you to your Lord Jesus Christ!*
>
> *And unto you a child is born . . .*
> *believe!*
> *He is the Child, your Lord Jesus Christ,*
> *who leads you to the Almighty.*
> *He is your truest friend,*
> *the one who dries your tears.*
> *He smothers you in His embrace*

and washes away your fears.
Cry for Him, your Christ who has risen,
for He will show you the way.
Have faith in Him, you mighty children,
for He is your true strength within.
We love you with all our hearts
and trust you are safe to believe,
for these are the words of God
we have given for you to receive.
Trust with all your hearts,
with everything you know to be true,
and you will be blessed with the multitudes of heaven,
and God's glory will reign down on you.
Go in peace, for you now have God's attention,
those of you who are here with us this day.
We look forward to witnessing your journeys,
for through His love you shall find your way!

Please hear me, O Lord, as I wait in my darkest hour,
for as I shine my faith to You,
You, my most Holy Spirit,
will shine Your magnificence on me,
for You are the Light of my salvation
that I look with my eyes to see! Amen."

*"Allow God to whisper the truth
upon your heart."*

MAY 18

The all-knowing of God

"Good morning, dear one. We wish to share a wonderful story with all. Please listen carefully so we may proceed. We love you with all our hearts!"

FOR ALL: *"Wherever you may go, Jesus Christ is always with you! Whenever you feel lost or down, He is the spirit which uplifts you and leads your return to the Father. He wishes to help all those willing to go far in their journeys. But you must know and remember . . . Jesus Christ is your leader on your path to righteousness. He has truly opened the door to your future, and it is now time for you to exercise your God-given rights and responsibilities in achieving your goals. Your belief in Christ alone is not the end to the All. As much as you would like this to be true, you must put your own foot forward. Do not fear! We do not wish to mislead you, for your welfare is our deepest concern. We will always lead you nearest the Father, and He so much wishes for you to understand that it is now time for you to take responsibility for your own journey. It is with the love, support, and guidance of your Lord Jesus Christ that you will attain your dreams and desires, yet also through your own motivations and actions. The road before you has been traveled by many, and you have much assistance waiting for you. You will learn a great many lessons in your journey, and you will become more enlightened with each passing day. Do not assume you can just ride the wave of time and be carried unknowingly to your rightful place with the Father, for He desires all to be knowledgeable in all aspects of His creation. And all must partake in His plan! No one can sidestep this journey, and no one's personal belief system can alter the Truth of the Universe. For there is only one truth, and it is the All-Truth of God. Whether you choose to believe and accept the All-Truth is left up to you, but you do not have the power to recreate through your own personal beliefs.*

It is now time for each of you to open your heart and mind to the Lord. Never assume you have all the answers, for no one upon this Earth can already see God's all-magnificence. You are only to remain open so God can orchestrate your knowing. Allow God to whisper the truth upon your heart. Listen intently, for He is your true guide. And as much as you might believe others have all the answers or are more knowledgeable of God's truth, the true knowing lies within each of you. And each of you brings to Him what you hold deep within. So it is your connection to God, and yours alone, which is the doorway to your destiny and your ultimate peace and heaven with the Almighty.

Listen to all you know and feel within your being. Look deep within and feel the presence of the Lord. Look to achieve your Oneness with the All-God, for He is the ultimate resting place of your soul. As you cross over from this existence, you will only carry on your way. And the relationship you have established will be your torch you carry beyond the boundaries of this world. You will leave behind those beliefs and attitudes of others, and you will be accompanied by only what you hold within your heart. Your God-connection will be the road map of your future. It will lead you further on your journey to the All-Knowing:

God is always with you . . .
God is always WITHIN you!

He is your answer . . .
He is the Truth that lies deep within
the CORE of your being!

You are the house of the Lord,
the embodiment of the All-Good of God;
you hold within ALL that is God!

You only need to truly see yourself,
and you will see God;
you only need to truly know yourself,
and you will know GOD!

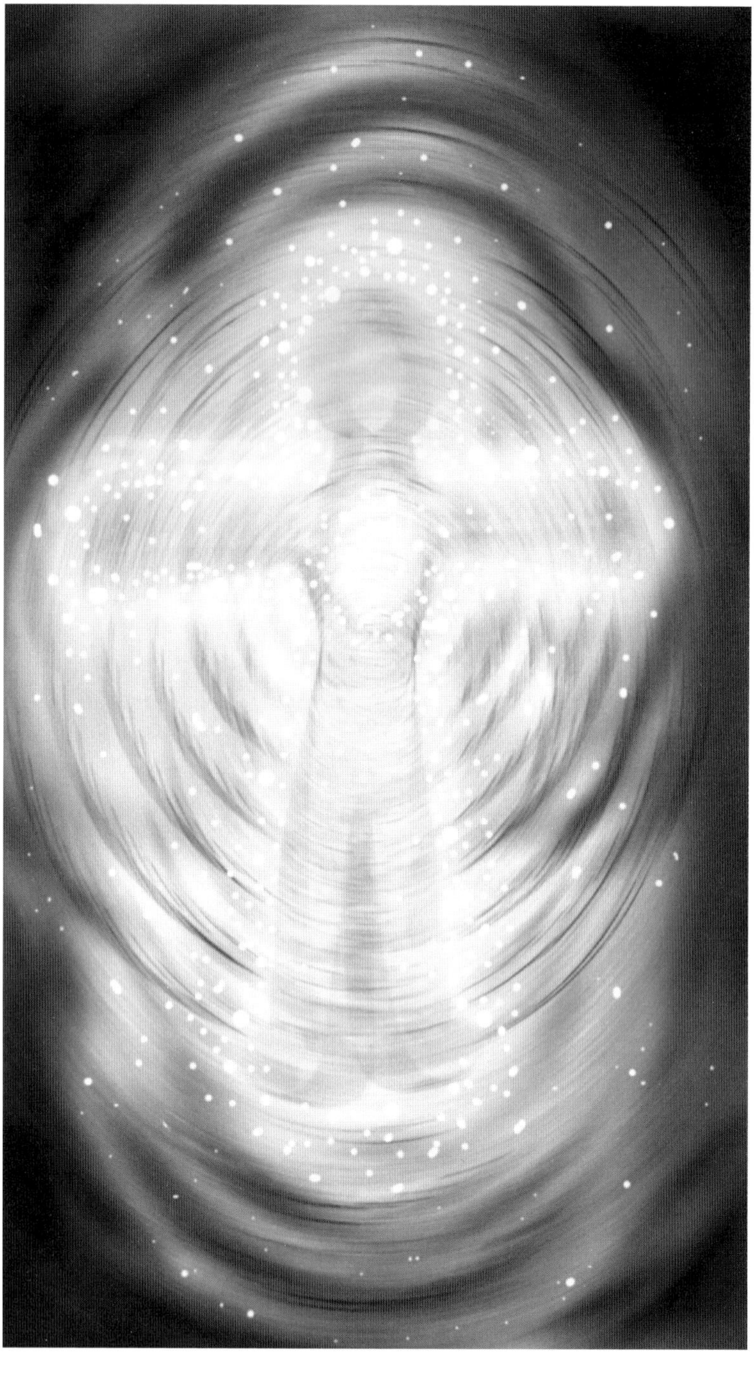

*As you acknowledge your true self,
the* ALL-TRUTH *is at hand!*

*Never doubt who you truly are;
feel the magnificence of* YOUR *being!*

As you seek to know, you will find . . .
BELIEVE!

As you CHOOSE *to unite with God,
you reunite with your true being!*

See all, be open to all, for heaven is upon you. It is the peace, the love, and the joy you behold when God reigns within. We bless you, we keep you . . . for YOU *are the Light of God! Amen."*

MAY 20

Spiritual growth

As I typed the latest message, "The all-knowing of God," for my notebook, I was aware of the gap in the dates between it and the previous message. I wondered if anyone else would make note of this. It's not that the communications of my angels stopped during this time but that they were for my personal guidance. I appreciated time away from the responsibilities of the book, since John and I had been preparing for a short vacation to San Francisco that we took this past weekend.

In the past I would have been more concerned about a lapse in time between messages, considering that when I first began receiving the messages for this book they came almost daily. I see as I glance back through the dates that the pace eased somewhat as time went on. This most likely was for my own benefit. Although I have been more than willing to do God's work and the changes in my routine have not been upsetting to me, even angels are aware that I—that we—need personal time. And why do you think this is?

I can remember that when my children were infants their growth spurts coincided directly with periods in which their daily sleep requirements increased. I am sure I read somewhere that children do actually grow in their sleep. Of course, I am speaking here of physical growth, and we as adults are no longer physically growing. But what about our spiritual growth? When do we grow spiritually?

When I look around, I see so many of us who fill our days with endless activities and commitments that we barely have time to breathe, let alone reflect on our lives. And we have come to accept and believe that if we are sitting still then we are wasting our time. I was taught growing up that work comes before play. Well, I know as an adult my work is never done. There is always something that needs my attention. So what am I to do?

I see my life from a different perspective than I used to, and I thank my angels for this transformation within me. It is through their guidance that I have become more aware of how we spiritually grow. On one particular day some time ago, I opened myself to receive a message for others, knowing it had been a few days since I had been given one and was concerned I might be losing touch. But what I believed would be given was not received.

> *"Dear one, you are trying too hard. Do not worry. We will take care of everything. Relax. Take time for yourself. Do not wear yourself out, for you then have no strength from the heart. Keep focused and tend to your needs. We will come to write with you another day. Do not feel sad. We just want you to be more rested. We love you!"*

I could not resist asking then what I could do to improve my life. Here is their reply:

"Just keep an open heart! God is here for you and is pleased you are so diligent, but He wishes for you to find more time for yourself instead of fretting over this book! Believe in yourself, and all will take care of itself. You tend to your needs. Enjoy the day. Do what satisfies you. Take a walk . . . get some fresh air . . . enjoy the breeze! Open to the goodness in all around you. You have so much to be thankful for. Do not assume anything! Enjoy the moment. Love all and others. Be sweet! We love you and wish you happiness. Look to this day with gladness. We will be here to enjoy it with you!"

What a divine message! I felt the entire day was given to me as a gift that I could spend however I chose. For the most part of the day, I just tended to odds and ends. When Ross came home from school, he invited me out to play basketball. I couldn't resist and out we went! We had a great time together. Some time later my youngest son, Andrew, arrived home from school and joined us. Eventually the game became more intense, and as I stepped off to the side to watch, my eyes were drawn to the woods. I couldn't resist taking a walk. All alone I went, just strolling through nature's greenhouse, absorbing the scents playing on the breeze and basking in the sun's rays that sifted through the foliage. And I realized that this was what I was meant to experience this day! I thanked my heavenly guides.

One day not long after I first began communicating with my angels, they commented on my welfare and also John's, saying:

> "You have not been getting enough sleep. You need time to renew your energy, time to relax and reconnect with your inner being. Others around you need this time also, especially John. He needs time to calm his emotions. He is just too busy concentrating on daily tasks and not nourishing his soul."

As my angels continued, they gave John this advice:

> "Listen to your inner voice, John. You tend to ignore it because it is easier not to listen, but you will see the joy it brings when you open your heart to it."

The message continued until it came upon these words:

> "You are being true to yourself and you are making great progress, but you need time to reflect on what you are learning. This is what spiritual growth truly is. Do not think your time is being wasted. Each day counts. Remember to pace yourself and acknowledge your spirit."

I did not realize at that time the significance of these words. If a child grows in his quiet moments, then do we as children of God also grow in our quiet moments? I know guidance comes to us constantly, but when do we take the time to notice? When do we quiet ourselves enough to listen?

I know that since my communications began my dreams have become more vivid and profound. I better understand their meanings and see how they apply to my daily life. They have been so enlightening. This is why I have chosen to share some of them with you. Could it be that they have always been this enlightening but that I just did not notice?

Then those little morning messages. Once I became aware of these words of wisdom, I could recall being given others in my lifetime. But in those instances, not yet understanding what they were, I simply dismissed them, letting them slip from my consciousness and allowing my controlled thoughts to take over. What guidance did I miss?

And what about that little voice within? How often do we stop to listen to it? Do we allow it to guide us, or do we *in our right minds* know better?

Help is all around us. When we choose to recognize it, to recognize its source, how can we then not choose to listen, to allow this wisdom to guide us? As we quiet ourselves, we open ourselves to listen. As we listen, we allow ourselves a chance to learn. As we learn, we can see and appreciate how we learn, and it is through our reflection that we also witness our growth. Through our openness we receive from God. It is then that we notice those little coincidences... those little miracles... those signs from God acknowledging we are on the right path!

Cherish your quiet moments, for they are not a waste of your time. Open to the guidance all around you. My early messages revealed:

"Pray for guidance. It will come to you."

"Learn to meditate. Find a time each day to receive guidance from God, the True Being of all light and love!"

"Take the opportunities given which show the Light... the Love... the Way. God blesses you each and every day. Be thankful! Open your heart and see even more!"

"Open your eyes! You will see and receive that which you desire. It is there for the asking. Remember, you must be aware to receive."

"Know you are loved by God. He is the force in your life that provides you with all you need and desire. Take the time to listen to His direction. He will never lead you astray."

"Calm your thoughts... open your heart... feel our presence! There are no boundaries, only your self-imposed limitations."

"Be open to all that comes to you, and so much will. It is there for the asking. We never doubt you will succeed. Let us help you! Always come to us with your desires to further your knowledge and understanding. We will help you in every possible way. We so enjoy our communications with you. It serves our purpose to help you in God's name."

❈

*"Only believe,
and you will surely be blessed
with His presence."*

❈

MAY 21

God's most glorious secret

*"There are many messengers
willing to do God's work."*

I am awakened. And, yes, it is still dark. But there is something different about this day. I can sense it. I can feel the excitement in the air. It is almost touchable, almost seeable . . . like a light . . . a shining light. I must calm my emotions and calm my mind. I must remember what I have learned. Take a deep breath and relax. Now, just open your heart . . . be still . . . and listen.

> FOR ALL: *"Love the FATHER! He is your giver of life, love, and true happiness. Never doubt He is in you. He is in all things . . . in all that moves to the rhythm of the Universe. There will come a day, should you choose to remain strong in your faith, that you will be blessed with God's truth . . . the All-Knowing of the Universe . . . the All within the heavens of your being! Choose to be open, and you cannot be but be blessed, and God's glory will reign down on you. You will go far in your journey, but you must always remain willing to*

keep a clear mind, and to be open to and accepting of all that speaks to your heart, for there is so much waiting to be revealed to you!

Never despair, for you will always be accompanied by your LORD JESUS CHRIST! He wishes to guide all those willing to go far in their journeys. We know it is hard for you to believe Jesus Christ could be so close at hand, for you cannot actually see His presence. But do not doubt, do not fear, for you will never be alone. Only believe, and you will surely be blessed with His presence!

Believe WE are here for you! There is much excitement among us, for we see the great adventure that lies ahead for you all. Do not despair, do not fear, for there are so many willing to guide. As you open to all around you, you will be moved by the power of the Universe. It is your heartbeat . . . your breath . . . the life force of your soul. It dances among the trees . . . sails down the sunny brook. Chases the raindrops . . . rests on the dew. It flutters beneath the wings of the songbird and makes its heart sing. Join in the glorious song of the Universe! Soar to the highest mountain! Your dreams can only be realized when you live them as truth. You can truly live in the Light of God. Look only within and allow its freedom. Let your light shine its glory to the heavens. Let God see your magnificence. For you are the reflection of His greatness . . . YOU are the mirror of His light and love! Never lose sight of this truth.

Go forward on this day! Only look into your heart and see, for the reality of your future lies within. You will only be blessed as you move forward on God's path. We have so enjoyed working with you and wish to end on a high note, for all good listeners deserve the best God can give. Listen as we share His most glorious secret!

Jesus Christ is surely with you! As you move forward in your journey, we cannot express enough His importance in your life. Look around you. Do you not feel His presence? He is with you as we speak!

> 'I am your Lord Jesus Christ, who has come upon this Earth in the name of Love so you may be of witness to the glory of heaven. Do not doubt My presence, for I am with you. Believe I come for you, and as I do, may you open your heart. Do not be afraid, for you will always be in God's mighty hands. Choose to follow His path . . . I will walk with you. Look forward to each day with gladness . . . I will be there. Look to each day with hope . . . I will be your strength. Never lose sight of your faith, and your measurable destiny will not be one of length!
>
> I wish always to present Myself to you in God's highest glory, as your welfare is My highest regard. Love, I send to you always. Believe, for it is I who writes with you. Open your eyes and see! I am your guiding light. I transmit your truth. Never fear, for I am always with you!
>
> Blessed be YOUR name in the eyes of our Heavenly Father! Amen.' "

MAY 22

We hear you

Dear heavenly guides, please help me to better understand what I have received in your latest message.

"Do not worry about what you receive, for you receive well! God does not wish to misguide. He loves you and cherishes your commitment. Believe we are here for you! Jesus Christ is here for you! God is always here for you!

You may now go forward with your book. Present it to those yearning for the truth, for there are many around you. We wish only to share what all are open to . . . that which allows growth. Anything else would not serve God's purpose.

Do not doubt, do not despair, for God is always with you. Believe in yourself, have faith in yourself, and all will come. You will be of witness to God's glory in your journey, for God wishes to bless you with His gifts all along the way!

We hear you, we hear your cry for help . . . and we always answer to your cries. Believe, and you will find yourself in paradise! Amen."

MAY 24

Great faith

Upon first receiving the words "I am your Lord Jesus Christ . . . ," I could not even begin to fathom their significance. Was Christ speaking directly to us, or were my angels choosing these words to express just how close He really is to us all? For you I cannot say. I can only present to you what I received. I know for myself, I am deeply moved!

    Soon after I received these words, all I could think was, *Why me?* for I was very aware of the doubt I could sense from the reader. But as I sat there trying to make sense of it all, I began to think, *Why not me? Why not me . . . or you . . . or you?* Why would we assume God and Jesus stopped talking to us all those years ago? Do we forget our worthiness to God? For those of you who might choose to doubt the source of these words, I would like to take you on a journey, one that I hope will help you make sense of it all.

    As I contemplated how you would accept these words, my thoughts traveled back to words contained within one of my early messages where my concern at that time had also been one of doubt, and I remembered:

> "Accept unconditionally what is given you. Does any of it not make sense?"

Well, in all the messages I have received, there has been nothing that has not made sense to me. In fact, there has always been a logic I cannot deny. Yet only yesterday I received a morning message that stated:

> "When you do not question what is before you, when you do not evaluate it for yourself, then you are not open to learning."

These two statements definitely seemed to be in direct conflict with each other. I was confused. There had to be some sense of reason here, however, for my angels have never led me astray.

After thought . . . study . . . reflection, I realized a truth. For when I returned to those early days in my journal to retrieve the message I thought I had accurately recalled, I found the words actually to be:

> "Do not doubt what you truly know and feel from within. Open your heart and accept unconditionally what is given you. Does any of it not make sense?"

So are we really to accept unconditionally what we are given, to never question if we know ourselves to be faithful believers? Yes, and no! When I received my morning message of yesterday, it came to me after I had spent the past two days seeking the truth through *outside* resources. My examination was of something that had *not* come from within. So when I read for myself the words "I am your Lord Jesus Christ . . . ," I can be comforted because I know they have come from within me, through me, and I have learned to trust what I hear, to trust what I feel from within. But what about you, for these words have not come from within you. They have come from outside of you. So, yes, you have every right to question and evaluate for yourself their truth as you have every right to question and evaluate anything that *ever has been* and *ever will be* presented to you. And how do you know what is true? It will speak to you. It will speak to your *HEART!*

When you have come to realize through your experiences that you can trust your inner voice, that it never leads you astray, and you understand that God is truly the voice that speaks from within, then you can accept unconditionally what is given to your heart. You can then believe without a doubt, and that is great faith! And a strong faith in God and in yourself allows you to question those things of your world, for you know in your heart you can trust what speaks to you. Faith means you accept that God directs you to the truth. Faith is trusting your inner voice, knowing it will lead you to the answers you seek. Through faith you move forward in your knowledge and understanding of God's truth!

Of all the lessons contained within the messages I have shared with you, the ones we cannot ignore are these: The truth lies within each of us, *and* when we seek God's truth, we will find it.

So *my* message to you is,

>Open your heart to the world around you . . .
>let your FAITH be your guide to the new world within!

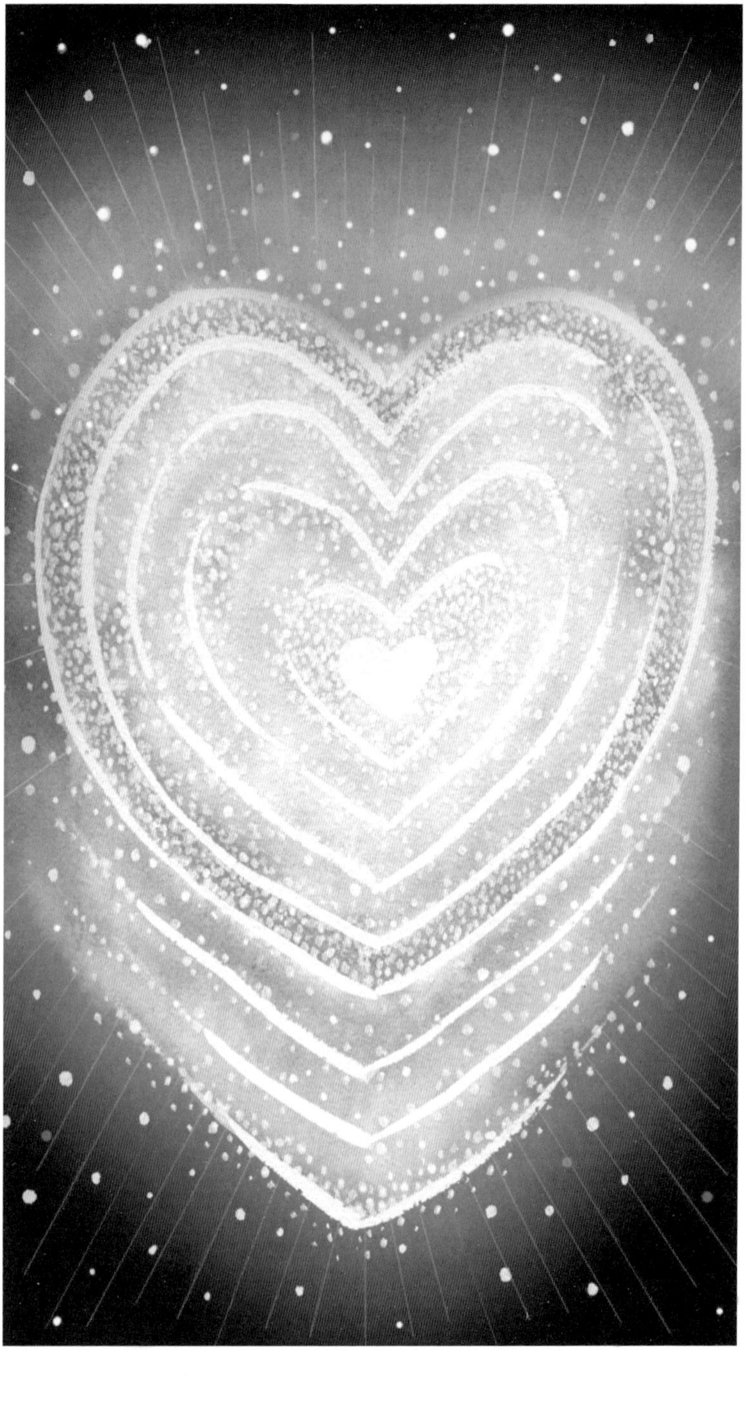

MAY 25

I AM

It is 4:40 A.M. and I am asleep. Still, a voice from within beckons. It calls out to be heard . . . softly, so quietly . . .

"I am the Truth . . . the Light."

From what source do these words come? Do not all things come from but one source? So I must ask each one of you, can we not all lay claim to these words?